SpringerBriefs in Sociology

More information about this series at http://www.springer.com/series/10410

Ulrich Dolata · Jan-Felix Schrape

Collectivity and Power on the Internet

A Sociological Perspective

 Springer

Ulrich Dolata
Institute for Social Sciences (SOWI VI)
University of Stuttgart
Stuttgart
Germany

Jan-Felix Schrape
Institute for Social Sciences (SOWI VI)
University of Stuttgart
Stuttgart
Germany

ISSN 2212-6368   ISSN 2212-6376   (electronic)
SpringerBriefs in Sociology
ISBN 978-3-319-78413-7   ISBN 978-3-319-78414-4   (eBook)
https://doi.org/10.1007/978-3-319-78414-4

Library of Congress Control Number: 2018935879

Translation from the German language edition: *Kollektivität and Macht im Internet: Soziale Bewegungen – Open Source Communities – Internetkonzerne* by Ulrich Dolata and Jan-Felix Schrape, © Springer Fachmedien Wiesbaden GmbH 2018. All Rights Reserved.
© The Author(s) 2018
This work is subject to copyright. All rights are reserved by the Publisher, whether the whole or part of the material is concerned, specifically the rights of translation, reprinting, reuse of illustrations, recitation, broadcasting, reproduction on microfilms or in any other physical way, and transmission or information storage and retrieval, electronic adaptation, computer software, or by similar or dissimilar methodology now known or hereafter developed.
The use of general descriptive names, registered names, trademarks, service marks, etc. in this publication does not imply, even in the absence of a specific statement, that such names are exempt from the relevant protective laws and regulations and therefore free for general use.
The publisher, the authors and the editors are safe to assume that the advice and information in this book are believed to be true and accurate at the date of publication. Neither the publisher nor the authors or the editors give a warranty, express or implied, with respect to the material contained herein or for any errors or omissions that may have been made. The publisher remains neutral with regard to jurisdictional claims in published maps and institutional affiliations.

Printed on acid-free paper

This Springer imprint is published by the registered company Springer International Publishing AG part of Springer Nature
The registered company address is: Gewerbestrasse 11, 6330 Cham, Switzerland

Contents

About the Authors

Ulrich Dolata is Professor in Organizational Sociology and Innovation Studies at the University of Stuttgart, Germany.
ulrich.dolata@sowi.uni-stuttgart.de

Jan-Felix Schrape is Senior Researcher in the Department of Organizational Sociology and Innovation Studies at University of Stuttgart, Germany.
jan-felix.schrape@sowi.uni-stuttgart.de

Chapter 1
Collectivity and Power on the Internet: An Introduction

Ulrich Dolata and Jan-Felix Schrape

Abstract The internet allows for collectivity to unfold into an impressive and multi-layered phenomenon that engenders diverse forms of entirely spontaneous or informally structured social behavior and action. The first aim of this book is to to present a heuristic concept of spontaneous collective behavior and directed collective action. Second, the book examines the role and importance of the technical infrastructures of the internet alongside the social rules embedded in those infrastructures for the formation, stabilization and structuring of collective action and behavior. The third concern of this book is to work out the different levels and facets of the power of the internet companies and their influence on the structuring of collectives.

Keywords Collective action · Collective behavior · Internet · Social movements Online communities · Socio-technical change

The internet has become an essential foundation of social action and behavior, opening up new or significantly expanded possibilities of communicating and taking action for both individuals and collectivities. This has resulted in mass phenomena such as customer feedback loops on shopping platforms such as Amazon; social networking communities (e.g., Facebook, Instagram, WhatsApp, Snapchat); media publication and consumption networks (e.g., YouTube); massive filesharing; and spontaneously evolving clusters of attention or outbursts of indignation on social media or around topics raised in hashtags (e.g., #metoo on Twitter). However, the mass phenomena also include organized interest and production communities in the context of the open source development of hardware and software (e.g., Linux kernel) or the development of free content (e.g., Wikipedia) as well as social movements that today utilize the social web as a matter of course when mobilizing and coordinating social protest.

This demonstrates that the internet allows for collectivity to unfold into an impressive and multi-layered phenomenon that engenders diverse forms of entirely spontaneous or informally structured social behavior and action. The *first aim* of this book is to capture and structure this diversity with an actor theory approach and to, on that basis, present a heuristic concept of spontaneous collective behavior and directed collective action in the digital era.

© The Author(s) 2018

U. Dolata and J.-F. Schrape, *Collectivity and Power on the Internet*,
SpringerBriefs in Sociology, https://doi.org/10.1007/978-3-319-78414-4_1

However, spontaneity and loose networking aside, collectivity never arises simply out of the blue. In all cases, it is embedded in specific institutional and infrastructural frameworks that have action-structuring and behavioral effects. These frameworks traditionally include institutional rules such as the right to assemble and demonstrate or the freedom of association; specific media infrastructures as platforms for information and communication; markets as arenas that shape and structure collective consumer behavior; or the presence of public spaces as places for people to gather either spontaneously or in a planned manner. The internet, then, comprises a new substantial layer of this infrastructure, namely one through which a significant part of today's social exchange is organized. Many individual and collective forms of information, communication and coordination have now moved into the online realm and are coordinated and channeled by a globally available set of manageable technical platforms and services. Facebook, for example, functions as a central social networking platform, WhatsApp as a major messaging service, YouTube as the crucial distribution hub for videos, Google as the central information search site, Twitter as a major messaging service, and Amazon as the leading web-based trading platform.

All of these platforms and services enable many new or significantly expanded forms of collective expression; however, they also structure and control them—often in rather rigid ways—through their technical specifications. The *second theme* of this book will focus on how exactly this takes place and examines the role and importance of the technical infrastructures of the internet alongside the social rules embedded in those infrastructures for the formation, stabilization and structuring of collective action and behavior.

The major platforms and infrastructures of the internet are today being developed and operated by just a few global technology companies—most notably Google, Facebook, Amazon and Apple. However, in addition to dominating the major commercial internet markets, these corporations also: function as the key gatekeepers and curators of individual and collective exchanges on the net; structure the communication and activity patterns of their users with their services; and, by doing so, have far-reaching infrastructural and regulatory powers that go far beyond monopolistic economic positions. That said, this does not make them omnipotent. After all, power is not an asset that some people have and others do not but always refers to a social balance of power that must be continually renegotiated. Overall, the currently leading internet corporations thus have to deal on an ongoing basis with volatile user behavior that can quickly and fundamentally question their business as well as with extremely dynamic market and innovation constellations, with rapidly emerging new competitors and niche dynamics, and with political regulatory efforts that aim towards a restriction of their influence.

Accordingly, the *third concern* of this book is not only to work out the different levels and facets of the power of internet corporations and their influence on the structuring of collective behavior but also to explore the relationship between power and volatility, that is, the (potential) fractures that could call into question their current status.

The four articles in this book examine in more detail the above-mentioned characteristics of and relationship between collectivity, infrastructures and power on the internet and summarize the research which the Department of Organizational Sociology and Innovation Studies at the University of Stuttgart has been conducting on these topics since 2013. More specifically, the articles look into:

- how different forms of internet-based collectivities—masses, crowds, movements, communities—might be understood and differentiated from one another using sociological actor and action theories;
- what role the technical infrastructures of the (social) web play for the formation, coordination and consolidation of those collectivities;
- how the mobilization and organization of social movements and social protests through the internet and social media have changed;
- how work, exchange and decision-making processes are organized in current open source communities, and why they are a far cry from comprising, as is the prevailing notion, a commons-based peer production;
- why the essential segments of the commercial internet are today concentrated in the hands of a few corporations who dispose over significant economic, infrastructural and rule-setting power.

In the *first article*, which deals with various forms of *collective action and behavior on the internet*, we make two basic distinctions. First, we differentiate between non-organized collectives and collective actors. Non-organized collectives, which include mass phenomena, crowds and episodic publics, are characterized by high situational spontaneity and do not have organizing, coordinating and decision-making structures that persist over time. For this reason, they are not discernible as independent social actors and instead constitute volatile forms of collective behavior. Communities of interest and production as well as social movements, on the other hand, can be understood as strategic collective actors who are shaped by cross-situational institutionalization processes. In the course of these processes, specific group identities, shared rules, conventions and goals as well as coordinating and organizing core structures emerge that then comprise the basis on which collective action that lasts beyond the concrete moment becomes possible.

In a second step, we examine the technical *infrastructures of the internet*, which today play an important role in the formation, stabilization and shaping of collective formations. Here we differentiate between widely used platforms on the social web, which are usually operated by market-leading internet corporations, and the formation-specific infrastructures that social movements and communities operate on their own. Non-organized collectives operate nearly exclusively on platforms such as Facebook, YouTube or Twitter, whereby they are subject to the technical specifications, algorithmic filter structures, terms and conditions, and rules of those platforms. Formation-specific infrastructures, by contrast, can be found in the context of open content or open source communities and online-oriented social movements. These two technical infrastructures not only have enabling features but are also characterized by rules and coordinating patterns that are embedded in the technology and that structure and channel collective as well as individual behavior. They also open hitherto unknown opportunities for social control and monitoring for private operators and government intelligence services.

In the *second article*, on *social movements*, the role played by the technical infrastructures of the internet today in the development and stabilization of protest is elu-
cidated in more detail. Its line of argumentation revolves around two themes. One
is the increasing degree to which the internet and social media affect the technical
foundations of collective action, by way of which they become not only connectivity-
enhancing infrastructures but also rule-setting institutions with a considerable scope
of intervention. The second theme explores, through a critical analysis of the popular
concept of "connective action," the novel and close interplay of social and technical
conditions under which collective protest and social movements take shape in the
digital age. We refer to this interplay as "technically advanced sociality," understood
to mean that the internet and social media do not replace the classical forms of protest,
such as street demonstrations or the occupation of places, but are, rather, embedded
in a considerably broader range of movement activities. At the same time, they are
not merely an additional element in the repertoire of contention either. As technical
and media infrastructures extending far beyond the scope of social movements, they
enable to achieve multiple networking and feedback processes in real time and over
the long term. They provide new opportunities for networking within and between
movements and contribute to the consolidation as well as the ongoing, long-term
feedback not only between activists and participants, and online and offline activities, but also between different media channels through which every social event
and social activity is directly shared, exchanged and returned to the movement or the
public.

The *third article*, on *open source communities*, discusses the changing relationships between established technology companies and open source-oriented software
development projects. To this end, the article engages in a systematic reconstruction of the differentiation of open source projects and their socioeconomic contexts,
followed by the presentation of four ideal-type variants of current open source projects—from corporate collaboration projects and elite-centric communities through
heterarchical infrastructure projects to a few egalitarian groups approaching the classic idea of commons-based peer production. Moreover, the text outlines that while
open source-funded software projects have largely lost their formatting as a counterpart to commercial production, they have, in contrast to previous types of collective
invention (i.e., the open and collaborative development of new technological structures), remained viable beyond the initial phase of innovation processes. Open source
software licenses, together with the coordination-facilitating features of the internet,
have established the sociotechnical framework for a permanent form of collective
invention. Initially, that framework was applied in subversive niches and later, starting in the 2000s, adapted from the commercial software industry as a complementary
development method. Today, open source projects have become important incubators for new product lines and fundamental infrastructures in a software industry
characterized by very short innovation cycles, as well as a fixed component of the
innovation strategies of all established technology companies.

The *fourth article*, which deals with the *internet companies*, examines the issue
of power in the online realm from a particular angle. The article analyzes the concentration processes taking place in the main internet markets as well as the expansion

and innovation strategies of the five leading companies Google, Facebook, Apple, Amazon and Microsoft. The findings presented in the text confirm neither any decentralization of market structures and democratization of innovation processes on the web nor any open and collaborative culture of technology and product development. Although today's internet economy includes the dispersed activities of countless start-up companies and developer communities, the commercial internet features a significant hierarchization and market concentration. At the same time, the commercial internet is characterized throughout by strong competition between the companies. This leads to a remarkable volatility of the acquired market and power positions, which must be repeatedly defended and renewed in the face of extraordinary innovation dynamics and volatile consumer preferences. Moreover, beyond dominating the commercial internet market, internet companies today have a more far-reaching hold on society. Given that they operate the web's key infrastructural foundations and serve as the main gatekeepers to the web, they have become the central rule-setting actors who structure the online experience of individual users and collective formations. More specifically, they impose framework conditions on these users and formations, whose movement and behavior emerges and takes shape around their offers and action. As such, they are not mere intermediary bodies, such as telephone companies, but have, through their infrastructural and rule-setting power, become leaders and opinion-makers in public discourse.

The articles featured here are based on discussion papers that were initially published in the *Research Contributions to Organizational Sociology and Innovation Studies* series of our department at the University of Stuttgart. For this book, all contributions have been revised and updated.

Stuttgart, Spring 2018
Ulrich Dolata
Jan-Felix Schrape

Chapter 2
Collective Action in the Digital Age: An Actor-Based Typology

Ulrich Dolata and Jan-Felix Schrape

Abstract This article investigates two questions: One, how might the very differently structured social collectives on the internet—masses, crowds, communities and movements—be classified and distinguished? And two, what influence do the technological infrastructures in which they operate have on their formation, structure and activities? For this, we differentiate between two main types of social collectives: non-organized collectives, which exhibit loosely coupled collective behavior, and collective actors with a separate identity and strategic capability. Further, we examine the newness, or distinctive traits, of online-based collectives. We consider that newness to be comprised of the strong and hitherto non-existent interplay between the technological infrastructures that these collectives are embedded in and the social processes of coordination and institutionalization they must engage in order to maintain their viability over time. Conventional patterns of social dynamics in the development and stabilization of collective action are now systematically intertwined with technology-induced processes of structuration.

Keywords Internet · Social media · Collective action · Non-organized collectives · Collective actors · Digital infrastructures · Socio-technical change

1 Introduction

From swarms and crowds to movements and communities, the internet allows for new forms of collective behavior and action anywhere on the spectrum between individuals and organizations. Online technologies allow for an aggregation of consumer preferences, which are compiled primarily from consumer feedback systems, or the extensive collective use of social media (e.g., Facebook, Twitter, Snapchat, Instagram) and file-sharing platforms (e.g., The Pirate Bay). Further collective phenomena include new forms of mobilizing and organizing political protests such as Occupy or Black Lives Matter as well as open content and open source communities such as Wikipedia or Linux. In all of these cases, online technologies seem to function as "organizing agents" (Bennett and Segerberg 2012, p. 752; see Bennett et al.

© The Author(s) 2018
U. Dolata and J.-F. Schrape, *Collectivity and Power on the Internet*,
SpringerBriefs in Sociology, https://doi.org/10.1007/978-3-319-78414-4_2

2017, p. 13) or at least as "technological tools that fundamentally enhance connectivity among people" (Bimber et al. 2012, p. 3). In that context, research seeks to identify any novel or inherently different social formations and agents on the web, many of which are considered to have far-reaching leverage to take action and assert influence.

So far, this search has remained unsatisfactory for two main reasons. One is the lack of sociological studies that better correlate the different forms of web behavior and web actions to actor and action theory and that go beyond the focus on individual cases or the presentation of trendy terms. Generic and otherwise loosely defined terms such as "swarm," "crowd" or "network" are regularly used as a catch-all for any new social formation that is not a stable social entity (e.g., Castells 2015; Ritzer et al. 2012; Ritzer and Jurgenson 2010; Benkler 2006) and tend to be accompanied by "ephemeral and apparently 'grass-roots democratic' conception[s] of collectivity" (Vehlken 2013, p. 112). Such notions contribute as little to an understanding of the vast range of collective activities on the web as does the similarly broad understanding of these phenomena as "undefined (and generally large) network[s] of people" (Howe 2006; see also Hammon and Hippner 2012).

In addition, apart from a few recent exceptions (e.g., Van Dijck 2013; Poell and Van Dijck 2016), sociological studies often fail to offer conceptualizations of the specific ways in which technical infrastructures impact the emergence, structuring and orientation of the different variants of online-centered social formations. Indeed, many studies do not go beyond general reflections on the relations between digital technologies and society (e.g., Graham and Dutton 2014) or the rather broad statement that most social movements in recent times were "born on the Internet, diffused by the Internet, and maintained [their] presence on the Internet" (Castells 2015, p. 171). While most of the literature points to the enabling character of the web (e.g., Bennett et al. 2014; Bennett and Segerberg 2012, 2013; Bimber et al. 2005), the formative role of its technical infrastructures in the constitution, structuring and operation of web-based collectives and their behavior is generally not addressed.

The key issues to be discussed in this conceptual article arise from these two deficits and are examined by posing the questions of (1) how collective formations on the web might be classified and differentiated based on actor- and action-based theory, and (2) what institutional role the technological infrastructures in which they operate play with regard to their development, structure and activity. In Sect. 2, we begin with a short review of basic sociological representations of collective formations and distinguish between two major variants: non-organized collectives and collective actors capable of intentional, strategic action. In Sects. 3 and 4, we apply this basic differentiation to our subject, distinguish between different types of online-based collective formations and discuss the significance of web infrastructures for their development, operation and stabilization. In Sect. 5, we present what we believe to be the distinctly new feature of online-based collectives, namely the unprecedented intertwinement of the, still required, social processes for the constitution, coordination and institutionalization of a collective with the technical infrastructures of the internet. In the online context, the classic social formation and organizational patterns of collective behavior or action mix systematically with discrete technological forms of structuration.

2 Basic Types of Social Actors

In order to understand the dynamics of web-based social formations and their structuring, organization, capacity and patterns of action, we begin by looking at existing actor and action concepts. In this chapter, we examine the heuristic and analytic value these concepts have for the study of new social collectives on the web. Three basic types of social actors that shape the realities of modern societies and that also operate on the web form the starting point of our deliberations: individuals, organizations and collective formations. These types of actors have different perceptions of reality, preferences, action orientations and decision-making modes and accordingly resort to different tangible and intangible resources for pursuing their goals (Scharpf 1997, pp. 51–68). Whereas individual and corporate actors represent relatively clearly defined units, the various collectives, on which this study focuses, are considerably more heterogeneous (Table 1).

2.1 *Individuals*

The ability of individuals to act intentionally and creatively as social actors is no longer disputed. Of course, the actions and scopes of action of individual actors are co-determined and influenced by the given social context, by social rules and norms, and by specific role expectations. By and large, individual action aligns itself with the orientations of regulatory, normative and cultural institutions; is subject to significant pressure to conform to a group; and is highly inclined to imitate behavior observed elsewhere or already regarded as socially positive.

Nevertheless, the actions of individual actors are not limited to the simple fulfillment of prescribed role expectations, the rigid focus on social norms and values, or compliance with well-defined rules, as was argued by the early proponents of structural functionalism (Durkheim [1885] 1970; Parsons [1937] 1949; Dahrendorf 1968). Rather, individuals are quite capable of consciously perceiving their personal and social environments and of offering their own interpretation thereof; of developing subjective, and often context-specific, preferences; of formulating their own goals for action; and of making their own decisions and following through with them (Turner 1978). In sum, acting individuals may be understood "neither as mere conformists nor as narrow-minded opportunists, but rather as more or less free, competent, creative and very emotional players" (Ortmann 2003, p. 133, our translation).

On the internet as well, individual actors set themselves apart by very different action orientations and different levels and scopes of activity and creativity. Each of them makes use of the expanded possibilities offered by the web in an independent and selective way. However, only a few of these actors intervene actively or creatively in the development of new technologies, products, services or content, make substantial contributions to the expansion of web services and infrastructures, or stand out for deliberately rule- or standard-defying behavior.

Table 1 Typologies of individuals, organizations and collectives

	Individual actors	Non-organized collectives	Collective actors	Corporate actors
	E.g., *users, consumers prosumers*	E.g., *masses, crowds, publics*	E.g., *movements, communities*	E.g., *companies, NGOs, NPOs*
Capacity for action	At the individual level	No independent capability for intentional, strategic action	Capable of intentional and strategic action beyond the participating individuals	
Resources for action	Individual resources	Situational aggregation of individual resources	Collective Resources contingent on the contributions of the participants	Organizational resources
Activity pattern	Individual	Collective behavior as aggregate of individual actions	Collective action on the basis of consensus, negotiation, voting	Corporate action on the basis of formal and hierarchical structures
Mode of decision-making	Individual decisions along individual preferences and goals	No collective decision-making capacity	Strategic decisions dependent on individual preferences of the participants	Strategic decisions independent of individual preferences of the members
Stability	–	Low	Context-dependent	High

Instead, the vast majority of individual web users use the new information, communication and consumer opportunities in the manner recommended by the respective web-based provider. For example, Facebook users wishing to be active on this social networking site can do so only within the confines of its technical parameters and by complying with its social etiquette, namely by agreeing with its terms and conditions—which they generally do without hesitation. This gives full rein to the behavior-shaping and norm-setting power of the internet and its possibilities: With all its applications, the web has significantly expanded people's individual possibilities for expression and their information and communication practices. Yet at the same time, it shapes individual action orientations as a new institutional setting that prescribes a regulatory frame for action. The impact of technology-mediated platforms and their social and technological rules on internet users is essentially that of orienting users' individual behavior, by far eclipsing the creative and independent participation of these users in the development of platforms (e.g., Fuchs 2017; Smith 2013; Lewis 2012).

That said, individual actors who use the internet primarily as offered to them can nevertheless have a social, political or economic impact through their actions and can influence processes or the concrete design of applications. However, this occurs only if and when their actions, be they individual preferences and forms of appropriation, concerns or resistance attitudes, consolidate into a mass phenomenon to which industry or politics must respond sooner or later. These include market-mediated individual consumer decisions as well as non-market exchange processes (e.g., file sharing) or non-organized resistance against offers, advertisement and data analysis practices on social networking platforms. This type of collective joint behavior develops in a largely uncoordinated manner and can be described as the contingent accumulation of similarly oriented yet often diffuse and malleable individual beliefs, understandings of problems, and usage and consumption patterns.

2.2 Organizations

However, modern societies are not primarily structured around individuals but are first and foremost shaped and motivated by the actions and interactions between formal organizations (March and Simon 1958; Coleman 1974; Perrow 1991). Much more so than individuals, corporate actors such as companies, political organizations or research institutes have the leverage to act systematically and reliably; have established and formalized action and decision-making routines; and have greater strategic capability when implementing their organizational resources, namely because they are largely independent on the preferences and interests of their members. Of course, they too are subject to the prevailing economic, political and social conditions. However, they are in a much better position than individual actors to, through their activities and resources, participate in the creation of the institutional foundation of their actions (Mayntz and Scharpf 1995).

For the analysis of structural patterns of new online-based collective formations, a look at organizations, in particular companies, is relevant in two ways. For one, large global corporations are the main drivers of innovative web-based communication technologies; and secondly, these technologies are then made broadly available to individual users as well as collective formations.

The five currently dominant internet companies—Apple, Google, Amazon, Facebook and Microsoft—each operate their own large-scale research centers, generally under top-secret conditions, and regularly present the internet community with new offerings. They expand their own innovative capacity primarily through far-reaching cooperation and acquisition strategies—such as the purchase of YouTube by Google, of LinkedIn by Microsoft or of Instagram and WhatsApp by Facebook. Of course, they must recognize and consider the often volatile user preferences and dynamics if they want to remain competitive. For this, they use data readily provided to them by the users themselves, and also draw on the creative potential of prosumers or "micropreneurs," e.g. in app stores for mobile devices (Dunkel and Kleemann 2013; Thackston and Umphress 2012). But at the same time, they manage to maintain control over their innovative activities and their core business (Dolata 2017). Even when hardware, software, services or content is developed by involving a large pool of users, this generally takes place under the direction of the dominant companies, who provide the framework for capturing and evaluating the impulses from these semi-professional contributors (Papsdorf 2009).

In that context, the leading internet companies are those that provide and develop the foundations of the web infrastructure. Typically, one or a few market-dominating companies control the central platforms that are frequented by individual web users and by many of the online-based collective formations. Apple and Google control the market for mobile devices, Google the search engine market and internet advertising, Amazon online trading, Apple, Netflix and Amazon the distribution of digital media content, and Facebook social networking—not only regionally but internationally. The dominant internet corporations are thereby regulatory actors who, by determining the sociotechnical framework for the movement of individual users, shape the online experience of these users and co-structure their collective behavior and action. In this way, mediated through the technical infrastructures which they themselves provide, they become main influencing factors of the formation and movement of social collectives on the web (see Chap. 5).

2.3 Collective Formations

The broad spectrum ranging from individuals to organizations features a great variety of collective formations. Such collectives may have very different coordination and movement patterns and cannot be indiscriminately regarded as social actors with shared objectives, resources and action orientations. In the following, we present what we believe to be the two basic types of social collectives, each of which exist in both the off- and the online context.

The first type consists of *non-organized collectives*, whose main attribute is the aggregation of similar decisions and behaviors among individuals. These collectives have no organized and action-guiding core, but have shared perceptions, approaches to consumption or ways of perceiving of problems, which may consolidate into a mass behavior. This phenomenon was identified as early as the end of the 1930s by Blumer (1939, p. 187), who maintained that: "The form of mass behavior, paradoxically, is laid down by individual lines of activity and not by concerted action." Blumer also pointed out (ibid., p. 187) that such a mass behavior can have far-reaching social effects: "A political party may be disorganized or a commercial institution wrecked by such shifts in interest and taste." However, such effects cannot be attributed to, as emphasized by Scharpf (1997, p. 54), deliberate or intentional decision-making of a collective actor but result from the similarly oriented behavioral decisions of individual actors: "The aggregate effect is then a result of individual choices, but it is not itself an object of anyone's purposeful choice." In other words, non-organized collectives do not act as one entity. Rather than constituting a rational and reflective entity of actors that makes deliberate decisions, they are characterized by spontaneous and volatile forms of *collective behavior*.

Such amorphous and rather random social constellations may then consolidate into social movements or communities that do have deliberately shared objectives, rules and identity attributes as well as more or less informal patterns of organization—in which case they represent *collective actors* capable of intentional, strategic action, the second type of social collective (see Chaps. 3 and 4). Over time, these formations develop a separate group identity, stabilize through institutionalization processes that allow for the reproduction of group structures, become differentiated internally between activists and hangers-on, and develop corresponding power asymmetries—which together gradually renders them capable of developing and implementing strategies and of mobilizing across a wide range of situations (Marwell and Oliver 1993; Eder 1993, pp. 42–62). Collective actors are characterized as having forms of organization that are specific yet nevertheless significantly different from formal forms of organization, as identified by Rucht (1994, pp. 70–98) with regard to social movements and by Dobusch and Quack (2011) with regard to communities. Neither social movements nor communities are "'non-organized', as they are based on implicit and explicit rules, their members share a conscious feeling of togetherness, and they form regularly around formal organizational units. However, in contrast to formal organizations, membership to a community is acquired […] through certain practices, decisions are made without reference to a binding legal framework, and there is no 'shadow of hierarchy'" (ibid., p. 177, our translation). Dobusch and Quack have termed this organizational pattern of collective actors as "organized informality," in contrast to the formal organizing in organizations. It is only when this organized informality becomes established that the respective formations become capable of developing and implementing strategies beyond the individual level and to move into the ranks of *collectively acting social actors*.

3   Non-organized Collectives and Collective Behavior

3.1   Types of Collective Behavior on the Web: Masses, Crowds, Publics

Many of the recent forms of more or less spontaneously arising collectivity (e.g., masses, crowds, mobs) are in principle no new phenomena for sociology. One of the first, and still inspiring, taxonomies of collective behavior was developed by the aforementioned Blumer (1939). He differentiates between three types of such behavior, each of which may transition into more stable forms of collective action.

The unorganized *mass* may be described, along certain criteria, as an aggregate of reciprocally anonymous individuals (Scharpf 1997, p. 53f.). Yet, as these do not consciously interact with one another, they do not give rise to concerted behavioral dispositions. Comprised of the users of sociotechnical infrastructures, recipients of mass media offers, voters and consumers, the unorganized mass may have, as a sum of individual choices, considerable influence on economic, political or technological developments; however, this influence it not collectively intended or deliberately staged. "Mass behavior, even though a congeries of individual lines of action, may become of momentous significance. If these lines converge, the influence of the mass may be enormous" (Blumer 1939, p. 187). The resounding success of Google as the preferred search engine, or of Facebook as the most popular social networking service, the rapidly growing recognition of the free encyclopedia Wikipedia, or the economic threat to media industries due to large-scale file-sharing—these are results of cumulative but not consciously coordinated individual choices. As such, they constitute genuine mass phenomena that operate without an organizing or orienting core.

The *crowd*, somewhat more delineated, does not have any pronounced coordination structures either; however, it differs from the mass through elementary forms of collectively-oriented behavior. This unfolds alongside nameable and often emotionally charged events, generating a temporary attention-grabbing field of tension without consolidating into a more solid form just yet. Disparate and self-reinforcing clusters of attention of a great number of individual online users, such as the multitudinous "likes" made to an entry, "clicktivism" in political campaigns, or waves of emotionally charged outrage on the social web—these are all crowd phenomena par excellence. They differ from the mass insofar as they display rudimentary features of event-related collective behavior.

Blumer also distinguishes masses and crowds from the *public*, which he defines as a "partial issue public" whose participants engage actively in discussions on a given topic and who exchange about their different ideas or suggested solutions: "[I]t comes into existence not as a result of design, but as a natural response to a certain kind of situation" (Blumer 1939, p. 189). In this respect, the spontaneously emerging yet rather ephemeral public differs from stabilized groups, which are not only characterized by organizational or cultural core structures such as communities or social movements but also by the ability to substantially co-determine the agenda-setting in situational public spheres (Schrape 2017). Temporary and barely regulated discussions about virally crystallized or mass-medially introduced topics on Twitter, social networking platforms or the general blogosphere—these are publics in the sense of partial issue publics.

All three of these variants of collective behavior are characterized by their volatility and spontaneity as well as the absence of distinct coordination and identity structures that go beyond a given moment. They are characterized by a *situational formation of the collective*, which generally dissipates after the event as rapidly as it appeared.

3.2 The Foundations of Collective Behavior: Infrastructures of the Collective

These classic distinctions of collective behavior allow to trace out and differentiate between non-organized web-based social formations more precisely than the very fuzzy analytical references to "fluid social networks" that prevail (e.g., Bennett and Segerberg 2012, p. 748). Yet, Blumer's set of distinctions fails to address two aspects that are of particular relevance in our context. First, the constitutive meaning of infrastructures for the creation, orientation and cross-situational reproducibility of collective behavior more generally and, second, the technological foundations that encourage and structure collective behavior more specifically. For Blumer, collective behavior develops unconditionally and spontaneously in largely unmediated and context-free situations.

By contrast, we hold that the outlined forms of collective behavior originate and evolve not without any conditions but rather in the presence of social and technical infrastructures that allow for the emergence of similarly oriented individual actions and the resulting collective behavior and that coordinate, guide, monitor and, to a certain degree, control those collective activities. We describe these *infrastructures of the collective* as institutional arrangements that enable the convergence of a collective in the first place and that, in addition, organize the circulation of information, ideas and people (Stäheli 2012).

Viewed from this angle, new forms of collective behavior result directly from the selective and individualized appropriation of already existing technological possibilities and infrastructures by their users. The many variants of non-organized collective behavior in the internet are strongly based on the there offered digital services and technical infrastructures, in particular the highly frequented social networking platforms.

- First, web infrastructures have *enabling characteristics*. The different web platforms expand the options for the procurement of information, facilitate the mutual observation of the behavior of other individuals, increase the interactivity and speed of collective forms of communication and exchange, and allow to communicate and take votes independently of location. All this facilitates the situational formation of non-organized collectives and expands their sphere of activity.
- Second, web infrastructures also develop *coordinating and regulatory characteristics*. The fixed and reproducible applications, functions, terms and conditions of their platforms not only contribute to the social structuring of non-organized collectives and collective behavior but also to their gradual stabilization. These structuring and coordination services, essentially provided by any web-based platform, are generally not developed by the user collectives (Van Dijck 2013).
- Third, web infrastructures are generating fundamentally new means of *social control*. Namely, they allow to observe, evaluate and judge (be it to sanction or to disapprove) motion profiles and preferences of individuals and non-organized collectives much more accurately and effectively than was previously possible. This control can be exercised not only by the private operators of the platforms but also by government intelligence agencies, who perform a near-total surveillance of user activities (Fuchs et al. 2012; Andrejevic and Gates 2014).

Empowerment, coordination and control—these are the ambivalent effects of the technological infrastructures of the web and its platforms on the formation and dynamics of non-organized collectives. Not only do they provide "technological tools that fundamentally enhance connectivity among people" (Bimber et al. 2012, p. 3), but they also have behavior-structuring effects and generate new means for the observation and evaluation of collective activities. In that sense, the technological infrastructures can be likened to social laws, regulations, standards or values that, as institutions that enable as well as structure and control individual and collective behavior, cannot easily be ignored or overridden (Dolata 2013, pp. 33–36; Werle 2011; Katzenbach 2013; Lessig 1999).

What is the reach of the structuring and coordination functions of web-based technical infrastructures? Is it possible for non-organized collectives to move beyond the mere aggregation of individual action and become collectively capable of action without having organizing core structures or social structuring activities of their own, in other words, through the behavior-structuring features of communication technology platforms alone? The works by Bennett, Segerberg and Bimber as well as related case studies (Bennett et al. 2014; Bennett and Segerberg 2012; Bimber et al. 2012; see also Anduiza et al. 2014; Carty 2015) suggest just that. Discussing Olson's (1965) *logic of collective action*, which emphasizes the constitutive role of incentive setting and coordinating organizations for the formation of collective action, these researchers hold that the traditional role of formal organizations can now occasionally be assumed by "digital media as organizing agents," which they refer to as *logic of connective action*: "Connective action networks are typically far more individualized and technologically organized sets of processes that result in action without the requirement of collective identity framing or the levels of organizational resources required to respond effectively to opportunities" (Bennett and Segerberg 2012, p. 750).

Although this matches closely with our understanding of non-organized collective behavior, the argument is problematic for two reasons. First, the generally available technical infrastructures on which the majority of individual action and collective behavior on the internet are based do not come from out of nowhere. Instead, these highly complex, costly and labor-intensive technologies are designed, offered, operated and maintained by a few leading companies. The currently dominant internet companies—Google, Facebook, Amazon and Apple—are increasingly those who provide and develop the foundations of the web infrastructure. Typically, one or a few market-dominating companies control the central platforms that are frequented by individual web users and by many of the online-based collective formations (Haucap and Heimeshoff 2014, 2017). These dominant internet corporations are thereby regulatory actors who, by determining the sociotechnical framework for the movement of individual users, shape the online experience of these users and co-structure their collective behavior and action. They channel collective behavior by means of social rules that are inscribed in the technology, and that often go clearly beyond mere technical requirements. Indeed, they provide incentives for certain behaviors and promote specific forms of communication while making others more difficult (Van Dijck 2013; Dolata 2017).

Thus, the technology itself only appears to execute, or implement, the coordination and structuring functions that enable collective behavior on the internet. The real protagonists are above all the leading internet companies, as these lay the foundations on which non-organized collective behavior on the web can unfold and become more stable (see Chap. 5). In this way, mediated through the technical infrastructures which they themselves provide as well as the "terms of service" of their platforms, they become the main influencing factors of the formation and dynamics of social collectives on the web and are assuming social structuring functions. For example, a shutting down of Facebook would have immediate and significant repercussions on all institutionalized forms of social communication, which are shaped and structured by the technical features of this particular social networking platform. As Van Dijck (2013, p. 37) rightly states, "all kinds of sociality are currently moving from public to corporate space," with a few companies acting as gatekeepers and defining the structures, rules and regulations the users have to follow as well as capturing and exploiting the data they provide—and they do so without any substantial democratic (i.e., public or political) participation and control.

Second, empirical evidence indicates that, on the internet, the transition from non-organized and volatile collectives to action-capable collective actors is likewise regularly accompanied by distinct *social* formation and differentiation processes and the emergence of more stable forms of organization and coordination. In particular the examples provided by Bennett and Segerberg (2012, p. 752) of *connective action*—open source software communities, Wikipedia or WikiLeaks—are not characterized, as one might think, by technically mediated and otherwise largely unorganized structures but are instead based on the distinct social features which we have referred to as organized informality (see Chaps. 3 and 4).

4 Collective Actors and Collective Action

4.1 Variants of Collective Action on the Web: Communities and Movements

The trend toward patterns of informal organization as a collective matures becomes evident when looking at more stable social formations such as *communities of interest* and *social movements*. They too have existed before the internet and have been an object of study in the social sciences for a long time.

A concept of community that goes beyond kinship or locally anchored classic communities was first introduced in the 1950s by Hillery (1955). In the subsequent decades, the term *communities of interest* was coined to refer to groups of people who are consciously and deliberately connected by shared views of reality or specific objectives rather than any geographical or friendship ties (Adler 1992). Such communities are neither based on any explicit hierarchical order, as exists with organizations, nor do they have a formal membership structure or binding rules of conduct. Nevertheless, as they mature, they generally begin to exhibit certain institutional characteristics, such as conventions, values, standards and knowledge structures, that shape the behavior of their members, mark the boundaries of the community, and foster a certain identity. Moreover, with time, specific coordination patterns and hierarchies emerge that stabilize the joint action (Cross 2013; Knorr Cetina 1999).

The internet is a perfect playing field for communities of interest in that the new web-based communication tools allow for coordination and collaboration independently of location. This too explains the emergence of numerous and diverse variants of online communities especially in the open source and open content domains. Among these are: *epistemic communities*, which Haas (1992) describes as a network of professionals with recognized expertise and competence in a particular domain; *communities of practice*, whose participants deal with similar (professional) tasks (Wenger 1998); *brand communities*, who share a sense of togetherness around a certain company or brand (Fournier and Lee 2009); and *subversive communities* (Flowers 2008), who use and develop technological infrastructures in unlawful ways for ideological reasons or for commercial gain. Their main commonalities are a thematic focus that goes beyond an ad hoc approach as well as the gradual institutionalization of a group identity with shared principles, conventions and rules among the active community participants, who operate projects of various kinds without a marked formal and hierarchical organizational structure (Mayntz 2010).

Similar to communities of interest, who focus on collaborative work and production processes, *social movements*, whose essential feature is collective protest, are not characterized by distinct boundaries. They are not held together through a formal membership structure, do not have binding and enforceable rules, and rely on continuous polling and consensus building among the participants (McAdam and Scott 2005). However, similar to communities, social movements do not operate without any structure or organization. Tilly and Rule (1965) conducted early research on how shared values and visions for change can lead to targeted collective action. For this they examined, aside from the political opportunity structures, the organizing cores of social movements, as they believed these to play a central role in a wide range of processes, ranging from the mobilization of resources to the emergence of identity models, the steering of protests and the recruitment of participants. As with communities, an increasing level of organization generally leads to internal differentiation in social movements as well—with opinion activists and coordinating core structures on the one hand and a broad network of supporters who can be mobilized on the other (Eder 1993; Rucht 1994).

Earl and Kimport distinguish between three forms of online-supported movements: *e-mobilizations*, for which the web is used primarily as a tool to facilitate the coordination of offline protests (e.g., street demonstrations); *e-movements*, where both the organization of the protest and the protest itself take place online (e.g., distributed denial-of-service attacks); and *e-tactics*, which combine online and offline components (e.g., petitions). It should be noted, moreover, that this ideal-type categorization serves more as a conceptual tool and that any one movement will most likely be a combination of two or all three forms, especially since online and offline protests generally overlap.

4.2   The Basis of Collective Action: The Institutionalization of the Collective

Despite their heterogeneity and diversity, communities of interest and social movements have three main features that distinguish them from volatile non-organized collectives and that raise them into the ranks of empowered collective actors: (1) institutionalization dynamics, which allow for, structure and stabilize collective action on the basis of their own, primarily informal, rules, norms and organizational patterns; (2) the building of a collective identity that orients the group's vision and actions and that defines its activities to the outside; (3) internal differentiation processes that, over time, spawn the emergence of organizing cores and opinion-leading activists, alongside their respective networks and support bases. While non-organized collective behavior develops on the basis of generally available infrastructures of the collective, a successive *institutionalization of the collective* is therefore typical of collective actors and collective action, which often finds its expression in independent organizing and structuring activities and services of the community or movement.

These institutionalization dynamics, which are part and parcel of the creation, consolidation and establishment of each community and movement, have traditionally been understood and analyzed as purely or primarily *social* processes, in other words, as the emergence of social rules, social identities, social organization patterns and social differentiations. By contrast, the role and significance of technical infrastructures for the institutionalization of collective actors and especially social movements has received little research attention until only a few years ago (Hess et al. 2007; Della Porta and Diani 2006; Davis et al. 2005). To be fair, this is not a failing of the academic community and results more from the fact that there was simply no need to deal with such matters for a long time.

Yet with the internet this changed significantly. Much of what distinguishes movements and communities—collective opinion-forming and voting, political campaigns and mobilization, organization and coordination of activities, professional exchange and collaborative production—has now moved into the online realm. Through this, the mentioned *social* characteristics of the institutionalization of collective actors are not overridden; however, their means of organizing and structuring their communications, production and protest are substantially expanded by the new *technological* infrastructures provided by the internet and its platforms. Accordingly, the institutionalization of the collective can today no longer be represented as a purely social but only as a *sociotechnical* process, understood as the systematic interweaving of social and technical structuring services, the interplay of which, however, varies greatly from case to case (Table 2).

Still today there are *social movements in the more classical sense* that, while utilizing web-based communication platforms to mobilize participants and coordinate their activities, nevertheless maintain significant similarities to their offline counterparts in their fundamental organizational modes and structures. Generally, they are carried by a series of activists, associations, NGOs and parties who cooperate on campaigns, plan thematically focused protest actions and implement these both

Table 2 Types of social movements and communities with online-leverage

	Main characteristics	Online leverage
"Classical" social movements e.g., protests against ACTA (2012) and TTIP (2014); G8 protests (e.g., 2001, 2007); G20 protests (2017)	Thematically focused protest actions; carried by a series of established actors (e.g., political parties, NGOs)	Partly utilizing web-based platforms for information and mobilization
Loosely networked movements e.g., Occupy (USA 2011); January 25 (Egypt 2011); Indignados (Spain 2011); Umbrella (Hong Kong 2014); Nuit Debout (France 2016)	Shared identity remains very general; (street) protests are organized by opinion-leading activists and social groups	Existing web-based infrastructures are widely used to communicate and organize
Internet-mediated issue generalists e.g., MoveOn.org (*1998); Campact (*2004); Avaaz (*2007)	Shared identity remains very general; great variety of political activities; organized by a small group of core activists	Use of a great variety of online and offline media to organize, support and disseminate political campaigns
Elite-structured groups e.g., Wikileaks (*2006); The Pirate Bay (*2003)	Focused on subversive activities; hermetically closed off core structures	Own technological platforms
Decentralized collectives e.g., Anonymous (*2004)	No organizing core; distributed operation by small units using a shared identity; meritocratic organizational patterns	Internal cohesion through formation-own infrastructures; public communication on Twitter, Facebook etc.
Production-oriented communities e.g., Wikipedia (*2001); Open Source Communities	Clearly defined collective identities and participatory structures; cross-cutting coordinating structures	Own technological platforms for collaboration and communication

offline and online. Moreover, leadership in the organization and coordination of activities is usually assumed by some of these actors (Earl and Kimport). Among such movements are the mass protests against the Anti-Counterfeiting Trade Agreement (ACTA) or the Transatlantic Trade and Investment Partnership (TTIP), which were coordinated and effectively publicized by a broad coalition of established left and green parties, NGOs such as ATTAC, clubs such as the Chaos Computer Club, and known web activists from the participating countries (Losey 2014; Verhoeven and Duyvendak 2017).

The above movements are different from *loosely networked movements* such as Occupy Wall Street or the Spanish Indignados, where the framework and shared identity that inform the organization of protest actions remain very general, and where web-based technologies and infrastructures like Facebook or Twitter are widely used to communicate and coordinate activities (Caren and Gaby 2012; Gerbaudo 2012).

That said, even here, despite the strong role of established social web services, the movements' formation, communication and mobilization has to depend on more than just the web infrastructures as such. These types of movements likewise have to rely on the mobilizing and organizing capacities of opinion-leading activists and established social entities—in the case of Occupy Wall Street, the Adbusters Media Foundation—who initiate the protests and bring them onto the streets. Such social cores are needed to stabilize the surrounding peripheries of following participants through the creation of cross-cutting coordination paths and overarching identities across a wide range of situations (Kavada 2015).

Moreover, there are *internet mediated issue generalists* that can be characterized as being both well-organized activist groups and social movements. They initiate and support a great variety of political campaigns, raise money for political candidates and organize many other activities ranging from e-petitions to street demonstrations and community meetings. Issue generalists such as the US-American public policy advocacy group MoveOn.org and its international counterpart Avaaz are based on small and well-organized activist core structures, additional campaign workers and large e-mail lists of supporters. Campaigning relies on their ability to flexibly use a great variety of media to disseminate their activities and to organize discussions. For this, they utilize their own e-mail lists and run campaigns using web-based platforms as well as traditional media such as newspapers, radio and television (Karpf 2012).

In addition, the internet has *elite-structured and clearly focused groups* that are characterized by subversive or illegal activities. Falling somewhere in between movement and community, these groups build their own technological platforms and have core structures and core actors, sometimes hermetically closed off, as well as support networks. A good example of such a group is WikiLeaks. A highly person-centered community, it has formed around a non-commercial organization that, nearly impermeable to influence from the outside, finds classified documents and makes them publicly available. Headed and represented by Julian Assange, it employs a very small team of employees and draws on a large pool of activists and supporters. However, the latter are not actively involved in decision-making (Roberts 2012; Davis and Meckel 2012; Brevini et al. 2013; Michael 2015).

By way of comparison, the internationally active *hacktivist collective* Anonymous, which carries out illegal cyber attacks of all kinds, is much more decentralized. Unlike WikiLeaks, it does not have an organizing core that is acknowledged by all participants, and the small units it operates are not necessarily aware of each other's presence. However, in and of themselves, these units are well organized and perform hacker attacks for which they publicly claim responsibility under the Anonymous label. Thus, they form different decentrally organizing cores of the movement. The movement maintains internal cohesion primarily through the formation-specific use of particular communication platforms (e.g., 4chan). Yet, this aspect of the movement is not egalitarian either. Here as well, meritocratic organizational patterns and their associated opinion leaders have emerged who dominate and structure the communication (Coleman 2014; Dobusch and Schoeneborn 2015).

Finally, in the open content and open source domain we now see very stable and infrastructurally independent *production-oriented communities*. These have not only developed their own and open technological platforms on which they collaborate and communicate, but also have clearly defined collective identities and clearly regulated and differentiated participatory, work and organizational structures. Such production communities are characterized, as shown in the example of Wikipedia, by two main features: One, they have cross-cutting coordinating core structures that culminate in the founding of an own umbrella organization (e.g., the Wikimedia Foundation), and two, over time they generate highly structured forms of self-organization at the operational level, with quality standards, work rules, control structures and a clear division of roles among the active contributors (Niederer and Van Dijck 2010; König 2013).

The above overview and the corresponding Table 2 are not meant to provide an all-embracing typology. Instead, they serve to strengthen and illustrate our argument and give rise to two observations: *First*, the *technical* web infrastructures have, despite their differences, become action-orienting and -structuring reference points for social movements and communities. The formation of new collective actors increasingly occurs through online-based communication and, often starting with little more than unstructured collective behavior, turns into organized forms of collective action. The internet is, therefore, now a major starting point of new social formations.

The internal structures of social movements and communities, too, are increasingly co-shaped by the web-based technical possibilities, the main ones being: new opportunities arising out of the removal of barriers to participation in collective activities, including their interconnection; an expansion of participants' radius of interaction and participation, including their possibilities to mutually observe each other; and greater transparency and control of the activities taking place in the organizing cores, which need to be promptly answered for and justified before the supporters. In addition, the new web-based technical possibilities constitute the foundation and structural basis for community-oriented work and production processes that would not be possible without the internet. Finally, the internet gives collective actors new means for shaping their image and visibility. It expands the possibilities for publicizing perceived grievances and influencing public opinion, and allows to facilitate the mobilization and networking of protests, and to increase the visibility thereof.

However, the online technologies thereby do not—which is the *second* point we wish to highlight—override classical forms of *social* organizing and structuring. Sustainable online-centered social movements or communities regularly resort to familiar social patterns of communicating and organizing in the course of their cross-situational stabilization and institutionalization (O'Mahony and Ferraro 2007; Dobusch et al. 2017).

- First, with time, collectively accepted social *rules, norms and values* take shape that have an influence on the orientation of a group's action. This applies to, for example, the editing and exclusion rules for Wikipedia entries or the collaborative work and production practices of open source communities. In this case, they evolve and manifest largely through web-based communication and structuring processes.
- Second, online-centered social movements and communities are characterized by the gradual formation of a *collective identity*. And as was the case with their offline

predecessors, a collective identity serves multiple purposes: It is reflected in the group's vision, ideology or mandate; often has a reach far beyond the group's activist core; forms the motivational point of reference for participants; has a mobilizing impact; consolidates collective action; and communicates the group's meaning to the outside.

- Third, distinctive although easily recognizable *organizational interrelations and core structures* develop that guide, coordinate and in part also control the activities of online-oriented social movements or communities. In the case of well-established communities in the web (e.g., open source project communities in the Linux realm), these interrelations and structures are often held together through independently operated technology platforms on which the bulk of the communication, opinion-forming and the actual work take place. As for social movements, loosely-networked activities occasionally transform into fully-fledged political parties (e.g., the Italian Five Star Movement or the Spanish Indignados).
- Fourth, in that context, more or less pronounced social *influence and power asymmetries* regularly emerge that arise from internal differentiation processes. Thus, online-centric movements and communities, too, are characterized by rather small activist cores (often with no more than 100–200 persons), who are largely responsible for the structuring and the output, and a far greater, in terms of numbers, periphery of participants and sympathizers who support the objectives of the formation and who can be mobilized around issues or projects (Gamson 2004).

The internet therefore does not lead to a disintermediation of genuinely social organization and structuring services. Instead, classic social organization patterns and institutionalization dynamics of collective actors mix with technological structuring services in new ways. The evolution of meta-individual intentionality, the emergence of a collective identity, and the development of informally coordinated rules and coordination structures—all of which transition situational and spontaneous collective behavior into cross-situational consolidated collective action—remain genuinely social processes. Thus, while the internet technologies can support the forming and stabilization of social movements and communities, the latter rely on much more than technology alone to build and maintain their momentum. Without tightly focused processes of social institutionalization, initially spontaneous emerging movements run the risk of turning out to be a flash in the pan and to lose ground as fast as they gained it, as can be seen in the decline of Occupy or the development of the oppositional movement in Egypt (e.g., Milkman et al. 2012; Alexander and Aouragh 2014).

5   Conclusion: The Socio-Technical Formation and Institutionalization of the Collective on the Internet

Our initial questions were: How might the different online-centered collective formations be classified along actor-based and institutional lines and what influence do the technical infrastructures in which they operate have on their formation, structure and activity?

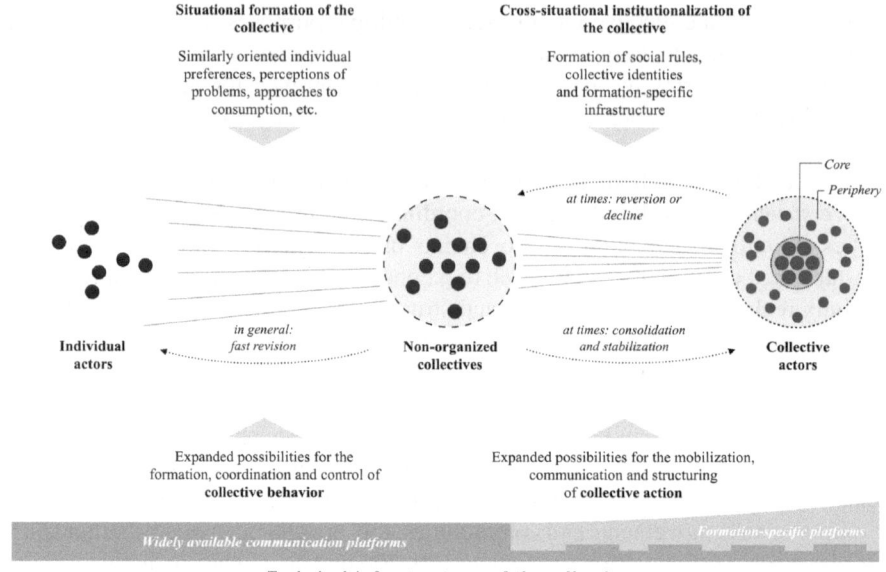

Fig. 1 Formation and institutionalization of online-centered collectives

With a view to their status as actor, social collectives can be distinguished into two basic types, each of which apply to both the off- and the online context (Fig. 1):

- The first type consists of *non-organized collectives*, such as masses, crowds or issue publics, whose activity is characterized by situational spontaneity and an accordingly high volatility. They have no own cross-situational coordination and decision-making structures and are not discernible as autonomous social actors but rather as spontaneous and volatile forms of collective behavior.
- The second type consists of *collective actors capable of intentional, strategic action*, such as communities and social movements, who are, by contrast, shaped by cross-situational institutionalization processes during which distinct group identities, shared rules and goals as well as coordinating and organizing core structures emerge that enable collective action.

What is unusual and specifically new about them in the online realm? This new consists, in short, of the significantly elevated role which technology—or, more specifically, technical infrastructures—plays in terms of the shaping, formation, operation and organization of collective behavior or collective action. Non-organized collectives and collective actors can no longer be described and summarized primarily with social categories, as was previously appropriate. Instead, they exhibit a close and novel interlinking of social and technological factors.

As infrastructures of the collective that did not exist previously, these technical systems and platforms do indeed facilitate the situational *formation of the collective*, in other words, the spontaneous emergence and operation of non-organized formations. They do so namely by allowing for reduced transaction costs and an accelerated speed of exchange, in turn enabling these formations to expand their range of action more readily. Through their rule-setting properties, web-based social media also contribute significantly to the structuring and cross-situational stabilization of both collective action and collective behavior, yet also to an unprecedented degree of observability and social surveillance, which is heavily exploited by the mostly private operators of the platforms and by state intelligence services.

In addition, as action-structuring and -orienting points of reference, the web-based technical infrastructures, in the form of commonly available or formation-specific platforms, contribute substantially to the cross-situational *institutionalization of the collective*. They generate greater visibility of collective expressions of behavior and action, which offers an ideal breeding ground for the formation of new collective actors with low-threshold opportunities. The web-based infrastructures also expand the patterns of interaction between the participants, contribute to the consolidation, organization and internal control of the activities of communities and movements, facilitate their external communication, and open up new possibilities for expressing grievances, exerting influence on public opinion and enhancing the visibility and mobilization of protest actions.

As inadequate as it may be to conceptualize and analyze web-based collective formations exclusively with social categories, it would be just as problematic to aggrandize technology or technical infrastructures into being the main and overriding factors of collective behavior and actions on the internet. This is because the very technological foundations in which collective actions take place reveal themselves to be genuine social processes—be it as new general offers and infrastructures developed by the leading internet companies or as independently-operated platforms that are created and further developed in the context of communities or social movements.

None of these web platforms on which people communicate, organize, work and mobilize is merely a technological offer that users can utilize or redefine as they please. Instead, social structuring patterns are already embedded in the platform technologies themselves. All technical specifications—not only those of commercial corporations but also those created by communities or movements—have rules, standards and action guidelines incorporated into them that influence the group's activities in a manner similar to social institutions and that (co-)structure the actions of their users in often very rigid ways. For instance, the presence of a clickable "like" button (alongside, as of 2016, five other reaction buttons)—and the absence of a technically just as easily implementable "dislike" button—on Facebook is not just a technical gimmick but a structural element of social rule-setting.

Processes of the formation and institutionalization of collective actors in the web, which generally transition successively from situational collective behavior into consolidated collective action, can indeed be sustainably supported and co-structured with communication technology. However, the fundamental structures and activities of communities or movements remain highly dependent on social conditions, which can be supported and shaped, but not substituted by technology. Among these conditions are: the emergence of a meta-individual identity and intentionality; the development of collectively accepted norms and values; the development of informal rules and coordination patterns; and the establishment of organizational structures and role differentiations. Technology alone cannot achieve that.

References

Adler, E. (1992). The emergence of cooperation: National epistemic communities and the international evolution of the idea of nuclear arms control. *International Organization, 46,* 101–145.

Alexander, A., & Aouragh, M. (2014). Egypt's unfinished revolution: The role of the media revisited. *International Journal of Communication, 8,* 890–915.

Andrejevic, M., & Gates, K. (2014). Big data surveillance: Introduction. *Surveillance & Society, 12*(2), 185–196.

Anduiza, E., Cristancho, C., & Sabucedo, J. M. (2014). Mobilization through online social networks: The political protest of the Indignados in Spain. *Information, Communication & Society, 17,* 750–764.

Benkler, Y. (2006). *The wealth of networks: How social production transforms markets and freedom.* New Haven: Yale University Press.

Bennett, W. L., & Segerberg, A. (2012). The logic of connective action. Digital media and the personalization of contentious politics. *Information, Communication & Society, 15,* 739–768.

Bennett, W. L., & Segerberg, A. (2013). *The logic of connective action: Digital media and the personalization of contentious politics.* Cambridge: Cambridge University Press.

Bennett, W. L., Segerberg, A., & Knüpfer, C. B. (2017). The democratic interface: Technology, political organization, and diverging patterns of electoral representation. *Information, Communication & Society.* https://doi.org/10.1080/1369118X.2017.1348533 (ahead-of-print).

Bennett, W. L., Segerberg, A., & Walker, S. (2014). Organization in the crowd: Peer production in large-scale networked protests. *Information, Communication & Society, 17,* 232–260.

Bimber, B., Flanagin, A. J., & Stohl, C. (2005). Reconceptualizing collective action in the contemporary media environment. *Communication Theory, 15,* 365–388.

Bimber, B., Flanagin, A. J., & Stohl, C. (2012). *Collective action in organizations: Interaction and engagement in an era of technological change.* Cambridge: Cambridge University Press.

Blumer, H. (1939). Collective behavior. In A. Lee McClung (Ed.), *New outline of the principles of sociology* (pp. 166–222). New York: Barnes & Noble.

Brevini, B., Hintz, A., & McCurdy, P. (2013). *Beyond WikiLeaks. Implications for the future of communications, journalism and society.* New York: Palgrave Macmillan.

Caren, N., & Gaby, S. (2012). Occupy online: How cute old men and Malcolm X recruited 400,000 U.S. users to OWS on Facebook. *Social Movement Studies, 11,* 367–374.

Carty, V. (2015). *Social movements and new technology.* Boulder: Westview Press.

Castells, C. (2015). *Networks of outrage and hope: Social movements in the internet age* (2nd ed.). Cambridge: Polity.

Coleman, G. (2014). *Hacker, hoaxer, whistleblower, spy: The story of anonymous.* London: Verso.

Coleman, J. S. (1974). *Power and the structure of society.* New York: Norton & Company.

Cross, M. K. D. (2013). Rethinking epistemic communities twenty years later. *Review of International Studies, 39,* 137–160.

Dahrendorf, R. (1968). *Essays in the theory of society.* Stanford: Stanford University Press.

Davis, G., McAdam, D., Scott, R. W., & Zald, M. N. (Eds.). (2005). *Social movements and organization theory.* Cambridge: Cambridge University Press.

Davis, J. W., & Meckel, M. (2012). Political power and the requirements of accountability in the age of WikiLeaks. *Zeitschrift für Politikwissenschaft, 22,* 463–491.

Della Porta, D., & Diani, M. (2006). *Social movements: An introduction.* London: Blackwell.

Dobusch, L., & Quack, S. (2011). Interorganisationale Netzwerke und digitale Gemeinschaften. Von Beiträgen zu Beteiligung? *Managementforschung, 21,* 171–213.

Dobusch, L., & Schoeneborn, D. (2015). Fluidity, Identity, and organizationality. The communicative constitution of anonymous. *Journal of Management Studies, 52*(8), 1005–1035.

Dobusch, L., Dobusch, L., & Müller-Seiz, G. (2017). Closing for the benefit of openness? The case of Wikimedia's open strategy process. *Organization Studies*. Online first. https://doi.org/10.1177/0170840617736930.

Dolata, U. (2013). *The transformative capacity of new technologies. A theory of sociotechnical change.* London/New York: Routledge.

Dolata, U. (2017). *Apple, Amazon, Google, Facebook, Microsoft. Market concentration–competition–innovation strategies.* Research Contributions to Organizational Sociology and Innovation Studies 2017-01.

Dunkel, W., & Kleemann, F. (Eds.). (2013). *Customers at work: New perspectives on interactive service work.* Basingstoke: Palgrave Macmillan.

Durkheim, E. [1885] (1970). *Regeln der soziologischen Methode.* Neuwied: Luchterhand.

Earl, J., McKee Hurwitz, H., Mejia Mesinas, A., Tolan, M., & Arlotti, A. (2013). This protest will be tweeted: Twitter and protest policing during the Pittsburgh G20. *Information, Communication & Society, 16,* 459–478.

Eder, K. (1993). *The new politics of class. Social movements and cultural dynamics in advanced societies.* London: Sage.

Flowers, S. (2008). Harnessing the hackers: The emergence and exploitation of outlaw innovation. *Research Policy, 37,* 177–193.

Fournier, S., & Lee, L. (2009). Getting brand communities right. *Harvard Business Review, 87,* 105–111.

Fuchs, C. (2017). *Social media: A critical introduction.* London: Sage.

Fuchs, C., Boersma, K., Albrechtslund, A., & Sandoval, M. (2012). *Internet and surveillance. The challenges of Web 2.0 and social media.* London: Routledge.

Gamson, W. A. (2004). Bystanders, public opinion, and the media. In D. S. Snow, S. A. Soule, & H. Kriesi (Eds.), *The Blackwell companion to social movements* (pp. 242–261). Maldon/Oxford: Blackwell.

Gerbaudo, P. (2012). *Tweets and the streets: Social media and contemporary activism.* London: Pluto.

Graham, M., & Dutton, W. H. (Eds.). (2014). *Society and the internet. How networks of information and communication are changing our lives.* Oxford: Oxford University Press.

Haas, P. M. (1992). Epistemic communities and international policy coordination. *International Organization, 46,* 1–35.

Hammon, L., & Hippner, H. (2012). Crowdsourcing. *Business & Information Systems Engineering, 4,* 165–168.

Haucap, J., & Heimeshoff, U. (2014). Google, Facebook, Amazon, eBay: Is the internet driving competition or market monopolization? *International Economics and Economic Policy, 11,* 49–61.

Haucap, J., & Heimeshoff, U. (2017). Ordnungspolitik in der digitalen Welt. In J. Haucap & Thiem, H. J. (Eds.), *Wirtschaftspolitik im Wandel. Ordnungsdefizite und Lösungsansätze* (pp. 79–132). Berlin: De Gruyter.

Hess, D., Breyman, S., Campbell, N., & Martin, B. (2007). Science, technology, and social movements. In E. Hackett, O. Amsterdamska, M. Lynch, & J. Wajcman (Eds.), *Handbook of science and technology* (pp. 473–498). Cambridge: MIT Press.

Hillery, G. A. (1955). Definitions of community: Areas of agreement. *Rural Society, 20,* 111–123.

Howe, J. (2006). The rise of crowdsourcing. *Wired, 14(6).* http://www.wired.com/wired/archive/14.06/crowds_pr.html. Accessed 1 February 2018.

Karpf, D. (2012). *The MoveOn effect. The unexpected transformation of American political advocacy.* Oxford: Oxford University Press.

Katzenbach, C. (2013). Media governance and technology. From 'code is law' to governance constellations. In M. Price, S. Verhulst, & L. Morgan (Eds.), *Routledge handbook of media law* (pp. 399–418). Abingdon: Routledge.

Kavada, A. (2015). Creating the collective: Social media, the Occupy movement and its constitution as a collective actor. *Information, Communication & Society, 18,* 872–886.

Knorr Cetina, K. (1999). *Epistemic cultures.* Cambridge: Harvard University Press.

König, R. (2013). Wikipedia: Between lay participation and elite knowledge representation. *Information, Communication & Society, 16,* 160–177.

Lessig, L. (1999). *CODE and other laws of cyberspace.* New York: Basic Books.

Lewis, S. C. (2012). The tension between professional control and open participation. *Information, Communication & Society, 15*(6), 836–866.

Losey, J. (2014). The anti-counterfeiting trade agreement and European civil society: A case study on networked advocacy. *Journal of Information Policy, 4,* 205–227.

March, J., & Simon, H. (1958). *Organizations.* Cambridge: Blackwell.

Marwell, G., & Oliver, P. (1993). *The critical mass in collective action. A micro-social theory.* Cambridge: Cambridge University Press.

Mayntz, R. (2010). Global structures: Markets, organizations, networks—and communities? In M. Djelic, & S. Quack (Eds.), *Transnational communities. Shaping global economic governance* (pp. 37–54). Cambridge: Cambridge University Press.

Mayntz, R., & Scharpf, F. W. (1995): Der Ansatz des akteurzentrierten Institutionalismus. In R. Mayntz & F. W. Scharpf (Eds.), *Gesellschaftliche Selbstregelung und politische Steuerung* (pp. 39–72). New York/Frankfurt a.M.: Campus.

McAdam, D., & Scott, R. W. (2005). Organizations and movements. In G. Davis, D. McAdam, R. Scott, & M. N. Zald (Eds.), *Social movements and organization theory* (pp. 4–40). Cambridge: Cambridge University Press.

Michael, G. J. (2015). Who's afraid of WikiLeaks? Missed opportunities in political science research. *Review of Policy Research, 32*(2), 175–199.

Milkman, R., Luce, S., & Lewis, P. (2012). *Changing the subject: A bottom-up account of Occupy Wall Street in New York City.* New York: The Murphy Institute, City University of New York.

Niederer, S., & Van Dijck, J. (2010). Wisdom of the crowd or technicity of content? Wikipedia as a sociotechnical system. *New Media & Society, 12,* 1368–1387.

O'Mahony, S., & Ferraro, F. (2007). The emergence of governance in an open source community. *Academy of Management Journal, 50,* 1079–1106.

Olson, M. (1965). *The logic of collective action. Public goods and the theory of groups.* Cambridge: Harvard University Press.

Ortmann, G. (2003). *Regel und Ausnahme.* Suhrkamp: Paradoxien sozialer Ordnung. Frankfurt a.M.

Papsdorf, C. (2009). *Wie Surfen zu Arbeit wird. Crowdsourcing im Web 2.0.* Frankfurt a.M.: Campus.

Parsons, T. [1937] (1949). *The structure of social action.* New York: Free Press.

Perrow, C. (1991). A society of organizations. *Theory & Society, 20,* 725–762.

Poell, T., & van Dijck, J. (2016). Constructing public space: Global perspectives on social media and popular contestation. *International Journal of Communication, 10,* 226–234.

Ritzer, G., & Jurgenson, N. (2010). Production, consumption, prosumption. The nature of capitalism in the age of the digital "prosumer". *Journal of Consumer Culture, 10,* 13–36.

Ritzer, G., Dean, P., & Jurgenson, N. (2012). The coming of age of the prosumer. *American Behavioral Scientist, 56,* 379–398.

Roberts, A. (2012). WikiLeaks: The illusion of transparency. *International Review of Administrative Sciences, 78,* 116–133.

Rucht, D. (1994). *Modernisierung und neue soziale Bewegungen. Deutschland, Frankreich und USA im Vergleich.* Frankfurt a.M.: Campus.

Scharpf, F. W. (1997). *Games real actors play. Actor-centered institutionalism in policy research.* Boulder: Westview Press.

Schrape, J.-F. (2017). Reciprocal irritations: Social media, mass media and the public sphere. In R. Paul, M. Mölders, A. Bora, M. Huber, & P. Münte (Eds.), *Society, regulation and governance: New modes of shaping social change?* (pp. 138–150). Cheltenham: Edward Elgar Publishing.

Smith, A. (2013). *Civic engagement in the digital age.* Report of the PEW Research Center.

Stäheli, U. (2012). Infrastrukturen des Kollektiven: alte Medien – neue Kollektive? *Zeitschrift für Medien- und Kulturforschung, 2,* 99–116.

Thackston, R., & Umphress, D. (2012). Micropreneurs: The rise of the MicroISV. *IT Professional, 3*(2012), 50–56.

Tilly, C., & Rule, J. (1965). *Measuring political upheaval.* Princeton: Center for International Studies.

Turner, R. H. (1978). The role and the person. *American Journal of Sociology, 84,* 1–23.

Van Dijck, J. (2013). *The culture of connectivity. A critical history of social media.* Oxford: Oxford University Press.

Vehlken, S. (2013). Zootechnologies: Swarming as a cultural technique. *Theory, Culture & Society, 30,* 110–131.

Verhoeven, I., & Duyvendak, J. W. (2017). Understanding governmental activism. *Social Movement Studies.* https://doi.org/10.1080/14742837.2017.1338942. (ahead-of-print).

Wenger, E. (1998). *Communities of practice: Learning, meaning, and identity.* Cambridge: Cambridge University Press.

Werle, R. (2011). *Institutional analysis of technical innovation. A review.* SOI Discussion Paper 2011-4. Stuttgart: Institute for Social Sciences.

Chapter 3
Social Movements: The Sociotechnical Constitution of Collective Action

Ulrich Dolata

Abstract For some years, the field of research on social movements has undergone fundamental changes. This is due above all to the internet and social media platforms that have become an integral part of the emergence, organization and mobilization of protest. This article examines the role which these new technical infrastructures play in the development and stabilization of political protest and social movements. For this, it pursues two main objectives: One, a more precise identification of the technical foundations of collective behavior and action, which show the internet to be not only an enabling but also a regulatory and action-structuring infrastructure with a considerable degree of intervention. And two, the analysis of the new and close interplay of social and technical conditions under which collective protest and social movements take shape in the digital age, referred to as "technically advanced sociality".

Keywords Social protest · Social movements · Social media
Connective action · Technically advanced sociality · Technology as institution

1 Introduction

For some years, the field of research on social movements has undergone fundamental changes with regard to its structure and orientation. More specifically, it has moved from conceptualizing and examining protest movements as purely social phenomena to taking into consideration the new technological foundations of collective action. This has been prompted above all by the internet and social media platforms that have come to play an integral role in the emergence, organization and mobilization of protest. Among the movements that were prominent examples of this trend are the Arab Spring, the Occupy protests, Movimiento 15-M in Spain, and the Gezi Park protests in Istanbul. As part of these developments, more research attention has been given to the role of internet platforms such as Facebook, YouTube and Twitter in the organization and mobilization of protest (Mason 2012).

© The Author(s) 2018
U. Dolata and J.-F. Schrape, *Collectivity and Power on the Internet*,
SpringerBriefs in Sociology, https://doi.org/10.1007/978-3-319-78414-4_3

In that context, especially the concept of connective action, developed by Bennett and Segerberg, quickly gained currency as a means to interpret these and other new social movements. The argument, in nuce, posits that in this day and age protest unfolds much more individualized and personalized than before and no longer requires the formation of action-guiding collective identities, strong leadership figures and conventional organizational structures. Instead, social media platforms, as organizing agents, are seen to take on the functions of coordinating and mobilizing protest. In that context, technologies, or more precisely the technical infrastructures of the digital world, then play a central role. They allow for new forms of protest, reduce the threshold for individuals to participate in protest, and serve as the main tool for organizing the protest (Bennett and Segerberg 2012a, b, 2013; Bimber et al. 2005).

However, the claim that social movements have undergone a full-circle transformation in the course of integrating mobilizing and organizing features of digital media has not been uncontested. There is, admittedly, consensus that social media have indeed broadened the scope of action and influence of protest. Nonetheless, so the counterargument, the new movements are still shaped to a considerable degree by offline activities, for example, by local strategy-building and organizational processes, local meetings, demonstrations in public spaces and face-to-face contacts. In addition, they too rely on identity-building processes and opinion-forming activists if they are to avoid disintegrating and having but a fleeting existence (Gerbaudo 2012a, b; Rucht 2014; Dolata and Schrape 2016)

Regardless of the degree of influence which the internet and its media platforms is deemed to have on social movements, most research contributions to this topic have one commonality: Despite the oft-made references to the action-enabling and action-expanding character of the new technological connectivity, the technologies themselves with all their embedded rules and regulations remain a blind spot in much of the discussion. Essentially, most studies do no more than simply acknowledge the presence of the internet and social media as technical offerings and infrastructures, often without ascribing any special rule-setting significance to them. "Technology is a tool, and therefore it is neutral" (Carty 2015, p. 5) is an apt depiction of this approach. Thus, the usage and behavioral rules embedded in the technical arrangements, their structuring effects, or the contexts in which they arise and the actors who develop and control them—all of these topics are not addressed in most research. Bimber et al. (2005, p. 384), for example, have stated that "our theory is agnostic about the origins of technology and the processes of social shaping that give rise to it and that influence the uses to which it is put."

Against the backdrop of this discussion, this article seeks to identify the role played by the internet and in particular by social media today in the development and stabilization of political protest and social movements. Following this introduction, the article offers a concise overview of the research on social movements and of the concept, somehow questioning the social component of said research, of connective action (Sect. 2). Section 3 pursues two tasks: One, to arrive at a more precise definition of the technical foundations of collective behavior and action, namely one that would reveal the internet and social media not only as enabling but also as regulating and action-guiding infrastructures and institutions that have a considerable degree of impact. And two, to assess the relationships between the technical and social conditions under which collective protest and social movements take shape in the digital age, referred to as "technically advanced sociality." Section 4 summarizes the core elements of the current-day sociotechnical make-up of social movements and discusses the prerequisites for a collective becoming a consciously acting actor. In other words, it examines how and when collective protest behavior that is initially spontaneous and largely uncoordinated transforms into a consciously conducted and strategically acting collective protest movement.

2 Social Movements: Conventional Categories, New Attributes and Blind Spots

2.1 Collective Action: Conventional Social Categories and Their Blank Spaces

In Western societies, social movements are everything but a new phenomenon. In the classic sense, they include the rather rigidly organized workers' movements that formed around distinct social milieus and that focused on economic conflicts. However, since the 1960s and 1970s, they also include new social movements that are structured like networks and that are oriented towards post-material values, such as the civil rights, anti-war, anti-nuclear power, ecological or women's movements. In that context, social sciences research on this topic likewise has a long tradition. In the United States, social movements began being an object of study as early as the 1960s, and in the German-speaking world since the mid-1970s (Goodwin and Jasper 2015, pp. 3–12; McAdam and Scott 2005; Rucht 1984). By now, social movements, as a topic, has become a recognized field of research within the social sciences, with findings published in a number of reference books (e.g., Snow et al. 2004a; Davis et al. 2005; Della Porta and Diani 2006, 2015; Goodwin and Jasper 2015).

The consolidation of this field of research, then, engendered a widely shared notion of what constitutes a social movement.

According to that understanding, a social movement is essentially (1) *collective protest* against perceived political, economic or cultural grievances. Social movements confront and challenge the ruling authorities, either demanding that a social transformation take place or seeking to prevent changes deemed unacceptable (Snow et al. 2004b). Nonetheless, a social movement is not usually referred to as such until its collective activities have consolidated into (2) processes of *cross-situational stabilization*. In this way, social movements are differentiated from more spontaneous forms of collective behavior or turmoil that tend to vanish into thin air after a singular action (Tilly and Tarrow 2015, pp. 7–12). "Social movement scholars have argued that contention that only lasts for a few hours or days is too much of a flash in the pan to be a social movement" (Earl and Kimport 2011, p. 183).

In the course of this stabilization, social movements also give rise to (3) specific forms of *social organization* of their activities. "There is absolutely no question about the fact that social movement activity is organized in some fashion or another" (Snow et al. 2004b, p. 10). Social movements are described, when differentiating them from the formal organizing taking place in bureaucratic organizations, as informal networks that are not held together through formal membership, that do not have binding and enforceable rules, and that instead rely on continuous and ongoing coordination processes between the participants (Della Porta and Diani 2006, pp. 25–28, 135–162; den Hond et al. 2015; Ahrne and Brunsson 2011). However, this is not to say that they do not have structure. In fact, they feature diverse patterns of "organized informality" (Dobusch and Quack 2011, p. 177; Dobusch and Schoeneborn 2015) that ensure the internal cohesion of the movement and that structure its external relations.

> In this case, "organizing" means establishing planning and decision-making structures, building communication channels and gathering the informal, motivational, material and cultural resources required in the confrontation with external groups. (Rucht 1984, p. 87) [our translation]

In that context, it should be noted that the increasing organization and stabilization of social movements is always accompanied by (4) internal differentiation processes, which manifest in the development of *leadership figures and organizing core structures* on the one hand and an environment of sympathizers capable of mobilization on the other. Leadership in the form of opinion-making and organizing activists is seen to have a decisive role in the development, consolidation (over the long term) and mobilization of social movements:

> It is the leadership which promotes the pursuit of goals, develops strategies and tactics for action, and formulates an ideology. The penetration of the movement in the society, the loyalty and involvement of its members, and the consensus of different social groups all depend upon the leaders' actions. (Melucci 1996, p. 332; Morris and Staggenborg 2004)

A last important feature of social movements that not only distinguishes them and stabilizes them across a wide range of contexts but that is also the object of intense debate in research on new social movements since the 1980s is (5) the formation of a *collective identity* that creates a sense of togetherness and a motive for action, and that manifests in the form of shared interpretive patterns, values, symbols, programs or guidelines. A movement's collective identity is engendered by the interaction processes between the participants of the movement; is always, given the heterogeneous social milieus from which participants hail, fragile and in need of continual revision; constitutes conceptual boundaries to the outside; and forms an essential basis for the movement's mobilizing capacity. In addition, the concept of collective identity explains why individuals engage in movements even if they do not stand to benefit directly from them, if the movement does not offer material incentives, or if the movement's chances of success are slim (Melucci 1996, pp. 68–86; McAdam et al. 1996; Della Porta and Diani 2006, pp. 89–113).

Protest, cross-situational stabilization, organized informality, leadership and collective identity—these are, in nuce, the main characteristics which the field of research has attributed to social movements since the 1980s. Until well into the 2000s, these characteristics were primarily conceived of as *social* phenomena and analyzed with regard to, for example, their role in the formation of social rules, social patterns of organization, social differentiations or social identities. By contrast, the role and importance of *technical* infrastructures for the emergence and institutionalization of social movements had received little research attention up until that time.

However, with the rapidly growing significance of the internet, this focus on social contexts and social conditions had become too narrow. After all, the processes by which collective opinions are formed or by which activities, political campaigns and mobilization are agreed on, organized and coordinated now at least partially also take place online. In that context, the challenge is to identify the extent of the impacts of these changed sociotechnical conditions on the emergence, development and actions of social movements. Does the extensive use of the internet and social media fundamentally change the foundations and the organizational and activity patterns of social movements? If so, does this point to the emergence, or existence, of a new type of movement that is characterized by the use of new technical arrangements and infrastructures and that can no longer be aptly described with the conventional attributes?

2.2 Connective Action: New Sociotechnical Attributes and Their Blind Spots

A relevant part of the more recent literature would respond with a yes to the above questions. The upsurge of a wave of protests at the beginning of the 2010s prompted a partly radical revision of the various conceptions of social movements. In that context, the focus was put on the enabling features of the technical infrastructures of the internet and the social media platforms, which were deemed to have far-reaching effects on the organization, coordination and mobilization of collective protest. The new movements were considered to be capable of doing without leaders and the formation of strong collective identities, and thus to be based on non-hierarchical and egalitarian structures. The coordination of these movements, it follows, could then be accomplished to a significant degree through the internet rather than by social movement organizations (SMOs) or organizing social cores. According to Carty:

> The Indignados, the Arab Spring revolutionaries, the Occupy Wall Street participants, and the DREAMers reinforce the declining relevance of existing SMO mobilizing structures, given the recent paradigm shift toward grassroots mobilization, spontaneous operation, leaderlessness, reduced reliance on money, and less labor-intensive approaches. (Carty 2015, p. 183; representative for many others, including Mason 2012)

The author continues to say that today's campaigns "tend to rely on decentralized self-organizing and flexible networks made possible through new communication flows and web-based tools" (Carty 2015, p. 183). Moreover, the new, individually and flexibly manageable online technologies aligned perfectly with the current network society, which is characterized less by stable social milieus and collective identities than by fluid, fragmented and personalized interpretive patterns and structures (Castells 2015).

The influential concept of connective action, developed by Bennett and Segerberg (2012a, b, 2013), Bennett et al. (2014a, b), is a prominent example of this reasoning.

> Connective action networks are typically far more individualized and technologically organized sets of processes that result in action without the requirement of collective identity framing or the levels of organizational resources necessary to respond effectively to opportunities. (Bennett and Segerberg 2013, p. 32)

According to this concept, technology becomes the focal point in the readjustment of collective action: "At the core of this logic is the recognition of digital media as organizing agents" (ibid. p. 35f). This means that the (mobile) internet technologies and, in particular, social media such as Facebook, Twitter and YouTube not only have a new communicative but also a discrete and far-reaching organizational potential.

> To an important degree, information and communication technologies become agents in connective networks, automating and organizing the flow of information and providing various degrees of latitude for peer-defined relationships. (ibid. p. 196)

From this point of view, the technical infrastructures of the web function as "*stitching mechanisms* that connect different networks into coherent organization," whereby they contribute to the stabilization of the new online-oriented social movements (Bennett et al. 2014a, p. 234). By contrast, classic organizational patterns, leadership figures and organizing core structures, as well as the development of a collective identity, a program or other types of action guidelines fall into the background. Connective action "does not require strong organizational control or the symbolic construction of a 'we'" (Bennett and Segerberg 2012a, p. 748; see also Castells 2015, pp. 246–271; Carty 2015). Instead, the initiation and dissemination of protest is increasingly done via social media platforms. The latter, then, are seen to stimulate spontaneous and non-hierarchical social protest largely without the input and structuring activities of movement organizations and without the necessity to construct collective identities. "Digital media platforms are the most visible and integrative organizational mechanisms" (Bennett and Segerberg 2013, p. 13; see also pp. 10–16, 45–52; Bennett et al. 2014a). This could be referred to as a *technical* constitution of collectivity, whereby the crowd no longer has to organize and transform into a movement on the basis of the above-mentioned *social* attributes in order to consolidate its protest activities over time.

This proposition is, of course, quite bold and far-reaching, provoking several questions. The first concerns the *role and characteristics of technology*, seen crucial for the constitution of new forms of collectivity according to the connective action concept. What constitutes the great and independent coordinating and organizing potential that is attributed to online technologies? By and large, the bulk of the new literature on social movements remains vague and unsatisfactory in providing an answer to this key question.

Admittedly, Bennett, Segerberg and others have repeatedly pointed out that the internet expands the options of information acquisition and dissemination; facilitates the mutual observation of the behavior of individuals; increases the interactivity and speed of collective forms of communication and exchange; and increases the threshold of individual participation in political or social activities. However, this alone does not suffice to characterize online technologies as organizing agents that are equipped with discrete structuring effects. If anything, they would qualify as, somewhat less stately, connectivity-enhancing infrastructures, in other words, as new means for the technical mediation of collective social activities. Understanding digital media as organizing agents—for which there is something to be said—would make sense only if the distinct characteristics of the technologies and platforms in question, including their regulating, coordinating and controlling impacts, were identified. However, the concept of connective action says almost nothing to this effect. There, technology remains, apart from the emphasis on its enabling characteristics and its connectivity-enhancing character, a black box.

A second question concerns the *relationship between the technical and social conditions* under which collectivity and protest take shape in times of digital media and the internet. In this day and age, can protest activity really be sufficiently maintained over time with the connectivity-enhancing and organizational features attributed to technology? Or does protest that does not want to remain episodic rely on genuine and labor-intensive social structuring and institutionalization processes even in the internet age?

Bennett and Segerberg (2013, p. 1) proceed to answer these questions by significantly limiting the scope of their concept.

> Much contemporary activism still resembles the familiar protest politics of old, with people joining groups, forging collective identities, and employing a broad spectrum of political strategies from street demonstrations and civil disobedience to election campaigning, litigation, and lobbying.

By this they are referring to social movements that are still today strongly influenced by the conventional patterns of movement organizations yet that now use the internet and social media as a complement to the mobilization and coordination of their activities. Castells (2015, p. 243) likewise points out that "it is essential to keep in mind that not all contemporary social protests are expressions of this new form of social movement. Indeed, most are not." Seen from that angle, a relevant part of today's social movements falls outside the scope of connective action and cannot be appropriately captured with the concept—something which tends to be overlooked.

Yet another question is whether the assumed new manifestations of connective action necessarily render obsolete the core characteristics that have traditionally been attributed to stable social protest and social movements—social organization, collective identity, leadership through opinion-forming activists and coordinating cores. Of particular interest here are the transitions from spontaneous and unorganized types of (mass) protest or upheaval, which have always been characterized by an initially diffuse and unstructured cacophony of moods, opinions and discussions, to more directed and sustained collective action. When do such transitions succeed, and when do they fail? What contributes to the stabilization of spontaneous mass activity? What role do the new technical infrastructures play, and how do they relate to genuinely social processes of structuring and institutionalization? Bennett and Segerberg (2013, p. 201), for their part, acknowledge that connective action networks have a "capacity, or at least a tendency, to adapt over time." However, they do not elaborate on this important question of how initially situational and unstructured collective behavior becomes consolidated, structured and institutionalized protest over time.

3 Social Movements and the Internet: The Transformative Capacity of Technologies and the Rise of a Technically Advanced Sociality

The shortcomings of the classic literature on social movements to integrate the new *technical* conditions for the formation of social movements into their conceptions are not really redressed by most of the recent literature on social media and protest. For one, although the recent literature does accord technology a central role, even deeming it capable of rendering genuinely social foundations of collectivity obsolete, it usually does not examine technology as such in more detail, whereby said technology remains a black box. Moreover, it hardly discusses the complex and dynamic interplay between new technical possibilities and *social* activities, which characterizes the emergence and stabilization, organization, structuring and mobilization of new protest movements.

The following aims to overcome these shortcomings. In a first step, the internet and social media are identified as new technical and media infrastructures that have not only facilitating and connectivity-enhancing properties but also rule-setting, regulating and structuring characteristics (Sect. 3.1). Whether, how and to what extent these new infrastructures are used is not considered to be technically determined, of course, but rather the result of genuinely social selection processes. In a second step, the distinct usage patterns of the internet and social media in the context of protest activities are described and typified as variegated processes of the social appropriation and embeddedness of these new technical possibilities in the action repertoire of movements (Sect. 3.2). In a third and summarizing step, the emergence, organization and dynamics of protest movements in the internet age is conceived as a sociotechnical constitution of collectivity that is characterized by novel interrelations between social and technical structuring patterns (Sect. 4).

3.1 The Structuring and Rule-Setting Capacities of Technology: Social Media as Infrastructure and Institution

Protest and social movements are always embedded in specific political, societal and social structures that influence their concrete possibilities, forms of organization and activities (Rucht 1984, pp. 291–323; Della Porta and Diani 2006, pp. 193–222). These contexts also include technical and media infrastructures that have always been adapted and used more or less independently by movements or that take shape as own contributions around collective activities.

Until the 1990s, movements had been increasingly making professional use of the telephone, telefax and conventional mail, as technical infrastructures, and of the mass media television, radio and print, as media infrastructures. At the same time, attempts were made to eliminate, at least partly, any dependencies on the publication strategies of the mass media through the launch of alternative newspapers (e.g., *Libération*, France, 1973; *tageszeitung*, Germany, 1978) or through initial experiments with self-produced video material and alternative television formats (Armstrong 1981; Boyle 1992).

The communication and media infrastructures available to social movements were relatively consistent and stable between the 1960s and 1990s (Croteau and Hoynes 2014, pp. 294–331). If anything, these decades saw a genuine *social* change, comprised mainly of the formation and establishment of a new type of social movement that reflected certain socio-structural shifts, cultural changes and the increasing importance of postmaterial values (e.g., the environment, civil rights, peace, gender)—all while remaining largely unconcerned and unaffected with technical innovations of any kind.

Starting with the 2000s, the protest and movement sector have been undergoing yet another set of changes. The latter are now significantly shaped by radical *technical* innovations and the attendant new communication and media infrastructures, which challenge the classic movements and their well-established organization and mobilization structures while allowing for new forms of expression and dissemination of protest. The visible surface of this new infrastructure is composed of the internet, as an ubiquitous and interactive information, communication and media network; social media platforms, as specific commercial services that by now provide the majority of user-generated content and private or public exchange on the internet; as well as multifunctional (mobile) devices such as smartphones, tablets or laptops, which serve as technical means of communication. The vastly invisible but essentially structuring foundation of this infrastructure consists of software applications of the most varied kind, which not only determine what can (and cannot) be done on the individual platforms but that also enable their operators to manage, aggregate and evaluate large volumes of data for their own purposes.

The extent to which these new multifunctional technical and media infrastructures may affect the formation and functioning of social protest and social movements is striking. They offer (1) new opportunities for the fast and easy documentation of perceived grievances or current events as well as the mobilization and viral dissemination of protest. The ubiquity of smartphones and social media such as YouTube, Twitter and Facebook (with WhatsApp) allow to post telling images, videos, emails or documents in real time; finding a broad audience, quickly, in conjunction with the use of classic mass media; and triggering spontaneous forms of protest without any major organizational effort. They also (2) open up possibilities for new low-threshold forms of protest. Among these are email campaigns, online petitions, wikis and discourses around hashtags, which like-minded people can launch or participate in without much effort, as well as new means to spread political manifestos and calls to action through social media. Furthermore, the new infrastructures affect the (3) established patterns of organization of classic movements in several ways. One, they have an impact on top-down mobilization and coordination, which can now take place online as well. Secondly, they engender expanded interaction and participation possibilities for the participants, as well as an increased transparency and control of the movement activities. Together, these impacts serve to relativize the power, or monopoly, which movement organizers have in determining the meaning, beliefs, strategies and guides for action (Earl and Kimport 2011; Earl et al. 2015; Vasi and Suh 2016; Crossley 2015).

Moreover, the internet allows for a (4) gain in autonomy through the establishment of movement-associated, media-mediated counterpublics. As a fundamentally open, decentralized and interactive infrastructure, it essentially offers room for building independent platforms on which news, pictures and videos can be published and disseminated as well as communicated and mobilized beyond both the traditional media and the commercial social media. In the 2000s, the alternative media platform Indymedia, which had emerged from the anti-globalization movement, was an attempt (albeit failed by now) to offer an independent counterpublic to mainstream media on a larger scale on the internet (Kidd 2003; McDonald 2015; Baringhorst 2009). Today, such autonomous forms of online counterpublics exist primarily in the context of top-down organized right-wing movements (e.g., the US news and opinion website Breitbart News).

The majority of the more recent literature cited in Sect. 2.2 focuses on the above-mentioned possibilities of the new technical and media infrastructures, yet overlooks (5) action-structuring and regulating features as easily as (6) novel control and monitoring capabilities that go hand in hand with the use of those infrastructures.

The sociological research on technology has long since established that technology invariably contains, embedded in it, rules, standards, instructions and control mechanisms, and that these have an impact on the activities of the users of that technology. As early as the 1970s, Linde (1972) attributed to technology (which he termed "things") a structuring (relationship-determining) as well as institutional (behavior-regulating) meaning, which he illustrated among others using the example of the assembly line in industrial production processes. In the beginning of the 1980s, Winner (1980, p 127f) characterized technological arrangements as structure-forming and regulating patterns of social order:

The things we call "technologies" are ways of building order in our world. [...] In that sense technological innovations are similar to legislative acts or political foundings that establish a framework for public order.

At the end of the 1990s, Lessig (1999) coined the famous metaphor "code is law," whereby he equated, on the basis of their behavior-regulating effect, all the instructions and procedures that are encoded in software with the law and other social regulating systems (see also Grimmelmann 2005). Popitz (1992, p. 31), for his part, also took a closer look at the contexts in which technology is developed and manufactured and pointed out that the action-structuring and -regulating features of technology are not simply there coincidentally but are instead deliberately designed and implemented by their manufacturers, who thereby have a regulating power.

[The power] is transferred, as it were, in materialized form to those concerned. That is to say, it is by no means a power of things over mankind—although it is suggestive of the ideology of "materialized" power—but a power of the manufacturing process and the manufacturers; a [...] power inserted by the manufacturer into the thing. (Popitz 1992, p. 31) [our translation]

In essence, these notions of *technology as institution* emphasize that technology and technical arrangements are never neutral and arbitrarily usable but always have structuring and regulating features that enable, channel and codetermine individual, organizational or collective action (Dolata 2013; Dolata and Werle 2007, pp. 17–22; Schulz-Schaeffer 2007). In contrast to social institutions, which take shape in the context of public discourse or political negotiations (where they also have to be legitimized), institutional inscriptions in technology are generally the domain of private-sector producers and are hardly ex ante negotiable or controllable. Of course, structures and rules embedded in technology are likewise, similar to social laws, regulations, behavioral norms or values, subject to interpretation and are constantly adapted, modified or invalidated by their manufacturers and operators as well as in the course of social disputes or unexpected user behavior. In principle, however, this does not alter the rule-defining and behavior-influencing characteristics of technology, by way of which said technology is elevated to the ranks of an institution.

With the internet, the institutional foundations and effects of technology have acquired a new quality. In particular commercially-operated social media platforms, which now host many online protest and movement activities, do more than simply represent "technological tools that fundamentally enhance connectivity among people" (Bimber et al. 2012, p. 3; see also Carty 2015, p. 5; Bennett and Segerberg 2012a). Indeed, this would be too narrow an approach. Rather, these platforms not only collect and exploit all the data that their users leave behind and ensure the seamless monitoring of their activities. In addition, their technical protocols, interface designs, default settings, features and algorithms structure and characterize the online activities of their users in a variety of ways.

Already, the predefined user interfaces and default settings of the platforms, which are not usually changed by the users, have a strong action-structuring effect in that they enable certain activities while excluding others. The embedding of features, such as the trending button on Twitter or the emoticon buttons and the trending news function on Facebook, are not just technical gadgets but regulating, action-orienting and opinion-forming elements. Indeed, they determine who or what is relevant for whom and what is not, namely on the basis of socially constructed algorithms. The latter serve to structure all information and interaction processes, anticipate user preferences, issue recommendations and, supplemented by the manual selections of content moderation teams, make decisions about what is obscene, objectionable, politically incorrect, erotic or pornographic—and proceed with the corresponding editing or deletion of such content. In this way, algorithms are highly political programs that construct distinct, selective and increasingly personalized social realities on the basis of social criteria that remain entirely nontransparent to the individual and the public (Gillespie 2014; Just and Latzer 2017; Van Dijck 2013, pp. 29–44; Pariser 2011).

Technology thereby becomes an organizing agent—albeit in a way that veers significantly from the concept of connective action. Social media platforms are not simply open technical infrastructures that can be arbitrarily used, redesigned and redefined by their users. While they enable new forms of individual and collective action, their technical specifications, functionalities and algorithms have a structural and behavioral impact, in the sense described by Linde, on their users. In essence, however, it is not the technical arrangements themselves but, following Popitz, the internet companies developing and offering them who are the actual organizing agents of online communication. As companies that like to see themselves as having a higher societal mission, they structure and shape large parts of private and public life on the web through the technically mediated social specifications of their offers—all below the radar of public perception and control (Dolata 2017). They are not merely intermediary instances, such as telephone companies, but are, through their infrastructural and regulating power, action- and opinion-forming "curators of public discourse" (Gillespie 2010, p. 347).

Given the extensive reach of commercially operated social media platforms, the latter are today used not only by individual users but also by protest and social movements, who then make less use of alternative platforms developed and controlled by themselves (Haunss 2015). The repercussions of the use of these social media offers for the purpose of political protests are more complex and ambivalent than any matter-of-fact listings of their enabling features might suggest.

On the one hand, the extended possibilities for action that have arisen with the use of the social web and its services and platforms are, paradoxically, accompanied by a significant *loss of autonomy of action*. This is because the dissemination and coordination of protest through social media must likewise adhere to the technical rules and specific functionalities of the platforms and the terms and conditions of their operators. As a result, the use of social media by social movements suffers a near-complete loss of control over their own data tracks, communication processes and content, which become the property of the operating companies in the context of this private-sector type of publicness. These companies evaluate, aggregate and algorithmically operationalize all activities, following which they mirror these activities back to the users in a selected form. Moreover, and importantly, if these companies deem the activities to be offensive or politically inopportune, they can also decide to exclude them. In this way, the selection logics of the classic mass media, traditionally deplored by the movements, are now complemented with the filtering and control mechanisms of the social media platforms, which are extremely opaque to users. By the way, this also means that the identities of many social movements—based largely on emancipation, criticism, openness, equality and self-determination—are confronted with a new media and technological infrastructure that is characterized by a near absence of transparency and a lack of public control (Leistert 2015; Hintz 2015; Poell and Van Dijck 2016).

On the other hand, social protest actions and social movements are, when using social media like Facebook, Twitter or YouTube, subjected to substantially *new means of observation and surveillance* which go far beyond the technical possibilities of the earlier days.

> When I supported the American protests against the Vietnam War," recalls Noam Chomsky (*Die ZEIT* 26/2013), "we did everything to avoid speaking on the phone. We knew we'd be intercepted. We only spoke openly when we were together in a small circle and knew each other. [our translation]

Indeed, the possibilities for observing and surveilling social media activities today are all-pervasive and seamless. This affects not only calls to action, manifestos or campaigns that are posted on these media but also all of the internal political communication and activities conducted there. The latter are systematically analyzed, condensed into people profiles and patterns of relationships, and arranged to be reconstructed and retrieved for years to come—both by the private operators of the platforms as well as, as has been known at the latest since the revelations of Edward Snowden, by state intelligence and security services (Andrejevic and Gates 2014; Lyon 2014; Bauman and Lyon 2013).

Overall, the transformative capacity of the new technical and media infrastructures on protest and movement activities is therefore considerable in various respects. Not only do the infrastructures open up new possibilities of dissemination, mobilization and organization but, given their regulating and behavior-structuring characteristics, they also intervene significantly in the concrete manifestations and possibilities of protest and render collective action observable and evaluable in a fundamentally new way.

3.2 Technically Advanced Sociality: Social Media and the Movements' Enhanced Repertoire of Action

The ways in which protesters and social movements deal with the internet and social media, the concrete usage patterns they form, how they integrate the new technical possibilities into their action repertoire, and the extent to which this impacts their activity and organizational patterns—all this is, of course, not technically determined but the result of genuinely social processes which cannot be eliminated with references to the organizing character of technology.

The sociology of technology has, as we have demonstrated, made the point that sociality in modern societies is a technically advanced sociality that takes shape not merely through social structuring and the interrelations of social actors but also through the action-orienting and regulating characteristics of their technical foundations. Indeed, contrary to the widespread notion that internet technologies and social media today play a central role in structuring new protest activities and movements, we want to argue that online-based forms of expression and organization are an important but not necessarily central component of movements' extended range of social activities. This becomes obvious when taking the broader social context as well as the variety of recent protest activity into consideration (see Table 2 in Chap. 2).

At one end of a wide spectrum are numerous new forms of *volatile online-mediated protest*, which are spontaneous, short-term and low-threshold and in which the use of social media plays a key mobilizing and coordinating role. The structure of this field is as heterogeneous as the organizing forms found there. The latter include purely online-based activities such as electronic petitions, email campaigns, online boycotts or political hashtag campaigns (e.g., #metoo), which are characterized by low participation thresholds and the online-mediated gathering of participants. They also include events receiving broad exposure and visibility (such as police brutality against blacks in the United States) that, disseminated via smartphones and social media, lead to spontaneous street protests; as well as calls to action and manifestos, issued by individuals or small groups, which can comprise the initial force behind the occupation of public spaces and demonstrations (as in Spain 2011).

Some researchers claim that these new forms of protest which are made possible by social media could be launched independently of movement organizations by so-called solo organizers or small teams without any organizational background (Earl and Kimport 2011, pp. 147–173). This is, however, only partly correct. Many email campaigns, electronic petitions or online boycotts, for example, no longer take shape spontaneously but are instead initiated and curated by professional campaign organizations such as Moveon.org, Campact, Avaaz and Change.org, who act as the selecting and coordinating cores of such activities (Karpf 2012; Dauvergne and LeBaron 2014).

These new online-mediated means of expressing protest do indeed allow achieving significant effects. They can trigger social debates, communicate displeasure, provoke social unrest and even spur far-reaching political activities. On their own, however, they cannot be characterized as social movements with a sufficiently stable degree of collective capacity for action. Instead, they might qualify as offering new means of expression and behaviors for a non-organized mass or crowd that is temporarily focusing its attention on a particular political or social theme or event. Such forms of initially volatile online-mediated protests often remain episodic, insofar as they usually disappear just as fast as it took them to emerge once the event is over (Dolata and Schrape 2016). However, they may insert themselves into the action repertoire of social movements, or set off an event that triggers far-reaching protest action of a newly forming movement (e.g., the Black Lives Matter movement; Dohrn and Ayers 2016).

At the other end of the spectrum, there are *strategically oriented and well-organized social movements* that do not differ fundamentally from their offline counterparts in their modes of action and coordination. What is characteristic for mass protests, such as those against the Anti-Counterfeiting Trade Agreement or the transatlantic free trade agreements TTIP and CETA, is that they forge broad social alliances with non-governmental organizations (e.g., Greenpeace or attac), clubs (e.g., Chaos Computer Club), professional campaign organizations (e.g., Campact or Avaaz), established left and green parties as well as individual activists, who plan and carry out thematically focused protests. As part of that process, a few of the involved actors, offices or campaign organizations usually assume leadership for the coordination of activities. The latter include, beyond the organization of street demonstrations and working with mass media, seizing and exploiting internet-based opportunities for expression and mobilization through their own websites, through social media platforms such as Facebook and Twitter, or through the launch of electronic petitions. Essentially, this constitutes collective action in the classic sense, insofar as it is considerably coordinated by movement organizations that have expanded their repertoire of contention by including the not negligible and systematic use of the internet and social media for exposure, mobilization and organization purposes (Losey 2014; Finkbeiner et al. 2016).

Apart from these well-organized movements and fluid forms of online-based protest behavior, other *more openly structured and web-based new social movements* also exist that rely significantly on social media platforms when planning and conducting their protest activities. Given their focus on the internet, they are often seen to comprise a new form of connective action. Among the examples of this type are the protests against the dictatorship in Egypt (2011), the Spanish 15-M Movement (2011), the Occupy movement (2011), the confrontations around the Gezi Park protests in Istanbul (2013), the Umbrella Movement in Hong Kong (2014) and the Nuit Debout movement in France (2016). As a rule, the activists and participants of this type of movement are recruited from the pool of well-educated, dissatisfied and online-savvy young people of the urban middle class. Their self-understanding is characterized by a deep skepticism of the classic forms of organizing and the propagation of informal, non-hierarchical and non-ideological structures. Moreover, these more openly structured and web-based new social movements were initially held together by a very general identity frame (e.g., "We are the 99%" or "Democracia Real Ya") without any further conceptual or programmatic specifications (Gerbaudo 2012a, b; Yörük and Yüksel 2014; Veg 2015).

Although these latter movements make systematic use of above all commercial social media platforms, in particular Facebook, Twitter and YouTube, they too are far more than connective action networks that organize themselves primarily over the internet. This becomes clear when the role of social media is exemplarily analyzed and reinterpreted in the now well documented movements to overthrow the dictatorship in Egypt, the protest of the Spanish Indignados and the Occupy movement in the United States.

In the weeks of the *overthrow of the Egyptian government* in early 2011, social media platforms, in this case especially Facebook groups, played an important initial role in the communication, mobilization and international visibility of the protest—albeit only for a short time. For example, the classic mass media, especially the television stations Al-Jazeera and Al-Arabiya, reporting continually and on site, soon became more important for the spread of the uprising within the country itself. Then, after the fall of the Mubarak regime, the urban online activists were suppressed yet again, this time by classic actors, especially the Muslim Brotherhood, anchored deeply within the society, and the military. Thus, in the political power struggle around the constitution of a new political order, the connective action networks no longer played a significant role—mainly because of their weak and fragile organizational structures, the political naiveté and inexperience of their activists, as well as the lack of programming and competence, especially with regard to economic and socio-political issues. In addition, this example, like the Gezi protests in Istanbul and the Occupy Central movement in Hong Kong, shows how easy and effective it is for the state security and police forces to monitor all online activities and to identify and pursue opinion-forming activists (Howard and Hussain 2013; Gerbaudo 2012b; Lim 2012; Aouragh and Alexander 2011; Alexander and Aouragh 2014; Gerlach 2016).

Social media activities also gave the impetus for *mass protests in Spain* in May 2011, namely against austerity, unemployment and corruption, which were not triggered by the established movement organizations. For example, the manifesto "Democracia Real Ya," which was the driving force behind the ensuing street protests and occupations, was written by individuals with no organizational background and was spread and discussed through a Facebook page. The latter subsequently became the main platform of the new movement and was shared by and connected to several hundred participating organizations, groups and blogs. However, while the start of the protests was almost exclusively carried by web-based discussions and activities, the role of social media decreased following the major demonstrations of May 15, 2011 and the ensuing occupations of public places. Although Facebook and Twitter were still used extensively, the essential communication and organization then moved from the internet to the actual meetings (*asambleas*) held on site and on the ground by the active participants. In addition, television and newspapers became increasingly important media for the spread of protests. The successful consolidation of the movement over time was based on two major social institutionalization processes that had little to do with social media. One, loose yet stable social networks of neighborhood meetings and local initiatives emerged, for example against foreclosures across the country. Secondly, the movement emboldened citizens to put themselves up for election and gave rise to the new party Podemos, which gave the movement a political program and direction as well as, through Pablo Iglesias, a charismatic leader (Gerbaudo 2012a, pp. 76–101; Castaneda 2012; Anduiza et al. 2014; Monterde et al. 2015; Iglesias 2015a, b; Simsa et al. 2015).

With the 2011 *Occupy Wall Street protests in the United States*, triggered by the banking and financial crisis, people vented their anger at the political system and their indignation at the blatant social inequality in society. The protests were kicked off by a professionally organized campaign of the consumer-critical journal *Adbusters* (which had also published the movement's initial call to action) and disseminated across various media channels. The movement's social media activities, in particular the use of Twitter and Tumblr, only became relevant during the course of the occupations—mainly for the mobilization, strategic coordination and dissemination of protests on the ground. Thus, in this case social media were of secondary importance for the initial organization of the movement, including the development of its cause and mission. Moreover, in spite of the movement's penchant for grassroots democracy, a small group of prominent opinion-making activists soon emerged. These not only organized the occupations, wrote the manifestos and served as the preferred media contact but also took command of the strategic use of Twitter, surrounded by a far greater number of more passive followers. The rapid decline of the Occupy movement and its low impact on politics can be largely attributed to its failure to become socially institutionalized. For example, the movement exhibited: a rather vague and broad orientation and a lack of programming, which benefited it only at the beginning of the protests; a refusal to cooperate with potential allies (e.g., trade unions or globalization-critical organizations), which was inducive to a certain navel-gazing of the protests on the ground; as well as a tenacious adherence of the participants to grassroots democracy, which impeded a more effective organization and more long-term stabilization of the movement (Gerbaudo 2012a, pp. 102–133; Milkman et al. 2012; Rucht 2013; Karpf 2014; Kavada 2015; Kneuer and Richter 2015, pp. 141–155). However, the Occupy movements' central demand for more social equality and justice in US-American society did regain some of its former status in 2015/16 in the context of Democrat Bernie Sanders' campaign for the 2016 presidential election, a campaign that was tightly organized and characterized by a strong online presence (Watkins 2016).

The examples show that the leading commercial social media platforms, especially, have become main hubs of protest initiation, mobilization and coordination at the latest with the social movements of the 2010s. However, even these new protest movements could not be characterized as connective action networks whose activities are predominantly online—at least not when considering that their undoubtedly strong online presences are, in turn, embedded within their numerous other activities, and when looking at not just their initial phases but also their development and their possibilities for consolidation over the long term.

What is typical of these movements, rather, is what I refer to as a *technically advanced sociality*, which is characterized by a novel and close interplay between socially based events, relationships, communication processes and activities and new forms of their technically mediated facilitation, dissemination and structuration. The use of the internet and social media is, as shown by the foregoing examples, a new and important but certainly not the only or most influential component of the activity profile and action and organizing repertoire of these movements. Thus, demonstrations, occupations, face-to-face communication and on-site strategy-building processes as well as the use of the traditional mass media do not become obsolete due to the use of social media.

Moreover, in the course of the cross-situational stabilization of initially spontaneous collective protests, genuine social institutionalization processes have a particular importance. These institutionalization processes include: the refinement of political demands and programs that have mobilizing and identity-building effects that reach beyond a given moment or situation; the capacity of the participants to form coalitions and networks of activities that stabilize and broaden the basis of the protest; as well as the formation of organizing core structures and opinion-forming activists that structure and choreograph the activities. It is only through such social institutionalization processes that initially spontaneous collective protest behavior can transform into a social movement capable of sustained, reflexive and lasting acting. Technology, by contrast, cannot deliver that.

4   Social Movements Revisited: The Internet, Social Media and the Sociotechnical Constitution of Collective Action

It would make little sense, however, to play out the (supposedly) new phenomenon of the internet and social media as organizing agents against the (supposedly) old social constitution of social movements. Instead, it is far more interesting and productive to explore the relationship and interplay of social and technical conditions of collectivity and protest in times of the internet, and to explore the concept of a technically advanced sociality of social movements. Overall, this concept can be summarized as follows.

The internet and social media have (1) sustainably expanded the *possibilities of expression of protest as well as the repertoire of action and organizational skills* of social movements. They have contributed to a remarkable pluralization of protest opportunities and activities; offer new actors such as individuals or small groups the opportunity to initiate protest; and create low-threshold access to protest activities, which allows to attract sympathizers and participants who are otherwise apolitical or not part of the more classic social movement environment. In addition, social media activities today play an important role especially at the beginning of protest waves, which are often triggered by attention-drawing and mobilizing online activities that can spread virally and in part independently of the traditional mass media (Bimber 2017).

However, despite all of these functions, social media are not removing the (2) *classic forms of social protest* from the playing field. Indeed, it is often through traditional activities such as street demonstrations or occupations that the whole thrust of a protest can unfold and become a substantial challenge for the established political practice in the first place. As a result, these activities will remain key components of the repertoire of online-oriented social movements as well (Gerbaudo 2012a; Della Porta 2014; Poell and Van Dijck 2016).

As soon as protest moves into these classic public spaces, (3) *face-to-face communication and on-site opinion- and strategy-building processes* gain in importance. Social media platforms such as Facebook or Twitter are used more to organize, to point to debates and discourses and to stir up emotionally than to develop, discuss and comment on content. Strategic decision-making processes, the planning of further activities or the writing of texts and calls to action still take place primarily in the protest environments on the ground, following which they are then communicated and disseminated via supporting social media activities, and via the traditional mass media (Kavada 2015, p. 880f; Haunss 2015, p. 26f, Kneuer and Richter 2015, pp. 170–184).

Especially television is still important for the continuous reporting of protest events and movements and has not yet been replaced by social media. What is typical, rather, is the (4) *increasing degree of differentiation within media infrastructures and the interdependencies between different media*, in which the internet and social media play an important but not exclusive role (Schrape 2016; Van Dijck and Poell 2013). Moreover, the use of social media by no means removes the, formerly often deplored, dependency of social movements on the media. The journalistic selection logics of the mass media are now supplemented by the algorithmic filtering, regulation and control logics of the commercial social media platforms. This not only influences the dynamics of collective perception and attention but also allows for the seamless and permanent monitoring and evaluation of these dynamics.

Thus, the internet and social media do not replace conventional forms of protest but are embedded in a considerably wider range of movement activities and repertoires. However, they are not merely any additional component in that repertoire. The real novelty is the omnipresent recursiveness generated by them: They enable, as technical and media infrastructures extending far beyond the scope of social movements, (5) *multiple networking and feedback processes in real time*. They provide new opportunities for networking within and between movements and contribute to the consolidation and to the permanent feedback not only between activists and participants and between online and offline activities but also between different media, through which every social event and every social activity can be directly exchanged, communicated and re-inserted into the movements' activities or the mediated public. With all this, the internet and social media form a new and distinct technically mediated structure and level of social protest action and have become an integral part of the technically advanced sociality of social movements.

Whereas social media can play a central role in exposing issues and as mobilization platforms in both spontaneous protest activities and in the early stages of emerging social movements, they are only partially suitable for the transformation of spontaneous collective protest behavior into strategically-oriented and persistent protest action of some political relevance. However, whether such transitions succeed primarily depends on genuinely social institutionalization processes. In other words, identity-building and organizing processes, which inevitably include accompanying social differentiation processes, remain constitutive of the collective becoming an actor capable of strategic and coordinated acting even in times of the internet and social media.

The focus on the consolidating force of technically-mediated connectivity underestimates the still existing (6) *necessity of substantial identity-building*, without which emerging social movements can neither be stabilized nor gain political influence over time as an extra-parliamentary voice. Very broadly kept umbrella identities such as "We Are the 99%," "Democracia Real Ya" or "Black Lives Matter" can trigger spontaneous protest but do not suffice to keep a protest going over time. The latter requires, to begin, the social competence for political coalition building and networking, without which protest remains isolated and self-referential. In addition, it requires the development of concretizing demands and a political program, which, as elements of a dynamic, meaningful identity, remain key prerequisites for the overall cohesion, the continuing mobilizing capacity and the relevance of a social movement within the political debate (Gerbaudo and Treré 2015). Bakardjieva (2015, p. 986) expressed this aptly as follows: "A depoliticized movement driven by connectivity […] may be good enough to help retrieve someone's lost mobile phone […], but not to challenge a government or a hegemonic cultural code."

Social media are, of course, not simply new media channels for the dissemination of manifestos, calls to action, demands and programs. Rather, they are also platforms where the exchange of individual perceptions and experiences is predominant and where political identity-building processes are much more visible, yet also less coherent, today than before, whereby they need to be continually re-communicated, re-negotiated and legitimized (Milan 2015). The new and difficult challenge for social movements today consists of picking up on the highly individualized protest behaviors and the elaborate cacophony of voices and moods, and to steer this towards a common political goal that goes beyond the moment.

This is not possible without (7) *social organizing structures and accompanying internal stratification processes*. Without the formation of organizing core structures and actors in whose surroundings activities are planned and coordinated, texts written, strategies developed, alliances made, and media attention generated, no spontaneous protest can be transformed into a long-term movement that is capable of action and strategy (Piven 2013; den Hond et al. 2015). This is, in fact, empirically observable and is typical not only of social movements in the more classic sense, where movement organizations still play an important role and where the organization of mass protest actions is done by specially set-up campaign offices. The new online-oriented movements and more volatile forms of collective protests too by no means function without organization and leadership. In fact, the initiation of electronic petitions, online boycotts or email protests is now often done by professional campaign organizations. Moreover, during protests on the ground, the more permanent among the new movements usually give rise to a certain division of labor and small informal groups of opinion-leading, media-savvy and well-connected activists who set the political course. This also affects the movement's social media activities, which are usually determined by a few key Twitterers with a large following and by the administrators of, say, Facebook pages, who play a key role as curators and choreographers of online communication. Gerbaudo (2014, p. 267) has referred to this as "digital communication teams, often bound together by links of friendship and comradeship who take the lead in initiating and steering relevant internet communications".

Such stratification processes, which can be evidenced everywhere, contrast strikingly with the non-hierarchical and grassroots self-understanding of many new movements. This is no new phenomenon (Morris and Staggenborg 2004). As early as the beginning of the 1970s, Freeman (1972) pointed out that even in such movements, whose participants deliberately want to do without explicit leadership, organization and decision-making structures, informal decision-making elites emerge who manage to remain unaccountable to anyone. Today, in times of a continuously mutual and media-based observation of activists and participants, such elites opt to function as soft and reluctant leaders who often want to remain anonymous and whose style of leadership is less commandeering and preaching than inviting and stimulating—yet whose subtle influence on the nature of the mobilization, coordination and communication of protest activities is nevertheless (or precisely for this reason) high (Gerbaudo 2012a; Poell et al. 2015; Kavada 2015; Karpf 2014; Treré 2012). Moreover, charismatic leaders in the classic sense, who mobilize masses and who hold movements together and shape their identity, have by no means disappeared from the movement scene but have been, on the contrary, experiencing a remarkable renaissance for several years now (Watkins 2016). Thus, the new movements are a long way from being free of hierarchies and leaders.

In order for the collective to become an actor, in other words, for the formation of a social movement that is capable of strategizing and taking action and that has a political impact that goes beyond the moment, far more is needed than technically-enabled connectivity. As a result, to become actors, collectives need to, still today, engage in genuine social institutionalization processes—something which technology cannot provide. Among these are the establishment of organizing structures, the formation of politically experienced activists, and the development of programmatic achievements and identity-building processes. Without such patterns of institutionalization, any protest or movement threatens to be just a flash in the pan and to remain politically irrelevant.

References

Ahrne, G., & Brunsson, N. (2011). Organization outside organizations: The significance of partial organization. *Organization, 18*(1), 83–104.

Alexander, A., & Aouragh, M. (2014). Egypt's unfinished revolution: The role of the media revisited. *International Journal of Communication, 8,* 890–915.

Andrejevic, M., & Gates, K. (2014). Big data surveillance: Introduction. *Surveillance & Society, 12*(2), 185–196.

Anduiza, E., Cristancho, C., & Sabucedo, J. (2014). Mobilization through online social networks: The political protest of the Indignados in Spain. *Information, Communication & Society, 17*(6), 750–767.

Aouragh, M., & Alexander, A. (2011). The Egyptian experience: Sense and nonsense of the internet revolution. *International Journal of Communication, 5,* 1344–1358.

Armstrong, D. (1981). *A trumpet to arms. Alternative media in America*. Boston: South End Press.

Bakardjieva, M. (2015). Do clouds have politics? Collective actors in social media land. *Information, Communication & Society, 18*(8), 983–990.

Baringhorst, S. (2009). Politischer Protest im Netz – Möglichkeiten und Grenzen der Mobilisierung transnationaler Öffentlichkeit im Zeichen digitaler Kommunikation. In F. Marcinkowski & B. Pfetsch (Eds.), *Politik in der Mediendemokratie,* Politische Vierteljahresschrift. Sonderheft 42 (pp. 609–634). Wiesbaden: VS.

Bauman, Z., & Lyon, D. (2013). *Liquid surveillance. A conversation*. Cambridge: Polity Press.

Bennett, W. L., & Segerberg, A. (2012a). The logic of connective action. Digital media and the personalization of contentious politics. *Information, Communication & Society, 15*(5), 739–768.

Bennett, W. L., & Segerberg, A. (2012b). Digital media and the personalization of collective action. Social technology and the organization of protests against the global economic crisis. In B. D. Loader & D. Mercea (Eds.), *Social media and democracy. Innovations in participatory politics* (pp. 13–38). London/New York: Routledge.

Bennett, W. L., & Segerberg, A. (2013). *The logic of connective action. Digital media and the personalization of contentious politics.* New York: Cambridge University Press.

Bennett, W. L., Segerberg, A., & Walker, S. (2014a). Organization in the crowd: Peer production in large-scale networked protests. *Information, Communication & Society, 17*(2), 232–260.

Bennett, W. L., Segerberg, A., & Walker, S. (2014b). Organizing in the crowd—looking ahead. *Information, Communication & Society, 17*(2), 272–275.

Bimber, B. (2017). Three prompts for collective action in the context of digital media. *Political Communication, 34*(1), 6–20.

Bimber, B., Flanagin, A. J., & Stohl, C. (2005). Reconceptualizing collective action in the contemporary media environment. *Communication Theory, 15*(4), 365–388.

Bimber, B., Flanagin, A. J., & Stohl, C. (2012). *Collective action in organizations. Interaction and engagement in an era of technological change.* Cambridge: Cambridge University Press.

Boyle, D. (1992). From Portapak to Camcorder: A brief history of guerilla television. *Journal of Film and Video, 44*(1/2), 67–79.

Carty, V. (2015). *Social movements and new technology.* Boulder: Westview Press.

Castaneda, E. (2012). The Indignados of Spain: A precedent to Occupy Wall Street. *Social Movement Studies, 11*(3/4), 309–319.

Castells, M. (2015). *Networks of outrage and hope. Social movements in the digital age* (2nd ed.). Cambridge/Malden: Polity.

Crossley, A. D. (2015). Facebook feminism: Social media, blogs, and new technologies of contemporary U.S. feminism. *Mobilization, 20*(2), 253–268.

Croteau, D. & Hoynes, W. (2014). *Media/society. Industries, images, and audiences* (5th ed.). Los Angeles/London: Sage.

Dauvergne, P., & LeBaron, G. (2014). *Protest Inc. The corporatization of activism.* Cambridge/Malden: Polity Press.

Davis, G. F., McAdam, D., Scott, W. R., & Zald, M. N. (Eds.). (2005). *Social movements and organization theory.* Cambridge: Cambridge University Press.

den Hond, F., de Bakker, F.G.A., & Smith, N. (2015). Social movements and organizational analysis. In D. Della Porta & M. Diani (Eds.), *The Oxford handbook of social movements* (pp. 291–305). Oxford: Oxford University Press.

Della Porta, D. (2014). Comment on organizing in the crowd. *Information, Communication & Society, 17*(2), 269–271.

Della Porta, D., & Diani, M. (2006). *Social movements. An introduction* (2nd ed.). Malden/Oxford/Carlton: Blackwell.

Della Porta, D., & Diani, M. (Eds.). (2015). *The Oxford handbook of social movements.* Oxford: Oxford University Press.

Dobusch, L., & Quack, S. (2011). Interorganisationale Netzwerke und digitale Gemeinschaften. Von Beiträgen zu Beteiligung? In P. Conrad & J. Sydow (Eds.), *Organisation und Umwelt. Managementforschung* (Vol. 21, pp. 171–213). Wiesbaden: Gabler.

Dobusch, L., & Schoeneborn, D. (2015). Fluidity, identity, and organizationality: The communicative constitution of Anonymous. *Journal of Management Studies, 52*(8), 1005–1035.

Dohrn, B., & Ayers, W. (2016). Young, gifted, and black: Black Lives Matter! In J. Conner & S. M. Rosen (Eds.), *Contemporary youth activism. Advancing social justice in the United States* (pp. 79–92). Santa Barbara: Praeger.

Dolata, U., & Werle, R. (2007). Bringing technology back in. Technik als Einflussfaktor sozioökonomischen und institutionellen Wandels. In U. Dolata & R. Werle (Eds.), *Gesellschaft und die Macht der Technik. Sozioökonomischer und institutioneller Wandel durch Technisierung* (pp. 15–43). Frankfurt/New York: Campus.

Dolata, U. (2013). *The transformative capacity of new technologies.* London: Routledge.

Dolata, U. (2017). *Apple, Amazon, Google, Facebook, Microsoft. Market concentration–competition–innovation strategies*. SOI Discussion Paper 2017-01. Stuttgart: Institute for Social Sciences.

Dolata, U., & Schrape, J.-F. (2016). Masses, crowds, communities, movements. Collective action in the internet age. *Social Movement Studies, 15*(1), 1–18.

Earl, J., & Kimport, K. (2011). *Digitally enabled social change. Activism in the internet age*. Cambridge/London: The MIT Press.

Earl, J., Hunt, J., Garrett, R. K., & Dal, A. (2015). New technologies and social movements. In D. Della Porta & M. Diani (Eds.), *The Oxford handbook of social movements* (pp. 355–366). Oxford: Oxford University Press.

Finkbeiner, F., Keune, H., Schenke, J., Geiges, L., & Marg, S. (2016). *Stop-TTIP-Proteste in Deutschland. Wer sind, was wollen und was motiviert die Freihandelsgegner?* Forschungsbericht Göttinger Institut für Demokratieforschung 2016-01. Göttingen: Göttinger Institut für Demokratieforschung.

Freeman, J. (1972). The tyranny of structurelessness. *Berkeley Journal of Sociology, 17,* 151–164.

Gerbaudo, P. (2012a). *Tweets and the streets. Social media and contemporary activism*. London: Pluto.

Gerbaudo, P. (2012b). The impermanent revolution: The organizational fragility of the Egyptian prodemocracy movement in the troubled transition. *Social Justice, 39*(1), 7–19.

Gerbaudo, P. (2014). The persistence of collectivity in digital protest. *Information, Communication & Society, 17*(2), 264–268.

Gerbaudo, P., & Treré, E. (2015). In search of the 'we' of social media activism: Introduction to the special issue on social media and protest identities. *Information, Communication & Society, 18*(8), 865–871.

Gerlach, J. (2016). Fünf Jahre Arabellion: Das Ende eines Traums? *Blätter für deutsche und internationale Politik, 61*(2), 47–56.

Gillespie, T. (2010). The politics of 'platforms'. *New Media & Society, 12*(3), 347–364.

Gillespie, T. (2014). The relevance of algorithms. In T. Gillespie, P. Boczkowski, & K. Foot (Eds.), *Media technologies. Essays on communication, materiality, and society* (pp. 167–194). Cambridge: MIT Press.

Goodwin, J., & Jasper, J. M. (Eds.). (2015). *The social movements reader. Cases and concepts* (3rd ed.). Chichester: Wiley Blackwell.

Grimmelmann, J. (2005). Regulation by software. *The Yale Law Journal, 114,* 1721–1758.

Haunss, S. (2015). Promise and practice in studies of social media and movements. In L. Dencik & O. Leistert (Eds.), *Critical perspectives on social media and protest. Between control and emancipation* (pp. 13–31). London/New York: Rowman & Littlefield.

Hintz, A. (2015). Social media, censorship, privatized regulation and new restrictions to protest and dissent. In L. Dencik & O. Leistert (Eds.), *Critical perspectives on social media and protest. between control and emancipation* (pp. 109–126), London/New York: Rowman & Littlefield.

Howard, P. N., & Hussain, M. (2013). *Democracy's fourth wave? Digital media and the Arab Spring*. Oxford: Oxford University Press.

Iglesias, P. (2015a). Explaining Podemos. *New Left Review, 93,* 7–22.

Iglesias, P. (2015b). Spain on edge. *New Left Review, 93,* 23–42.

Just, N., & Latzer, M. (2017). Governance by algorithms: Reality construction by algorithmic selection on the internet. *Media, Culture and Society, 39*(2), 238–258.

Karpf, D. (2012). *The MoveOn effect. Transformation of American political advocacy*. Oxford: Oxford University Press.

Karpf, D. (2014). Comment on "Organization in the crowd: Peer production in large-scale networked protests". *Information, Communication & Society, 17*(2), 261–263.

Kavada, A. (2015). Creating the collective: Social media, the Occupy movement and its constitution as a collective actor. *Information, Communication & Society, 18*(8), 872–886.

Kidd, D. (2003). Indymedia.org. A new communications commons. In M. McCaughey & M. Dyers (Eds.), *Cyberactivism: Online activism in theory and practice* (pp. 47–69). New York: Routledge.

Kneuer, M., & Richter, S. (2015). *Soziale Medien in Protestbewegungen. Neue Wege für Diskurs, Organisation und Empörung?* Frankfurt/New York: Campus.

Leistert, O. (2015). The revolution will not be liked. In L. Dencik & O. Leistert (Eds.), *Critical perspectives on social media and protest. Between control and emancipation* (pp. 35–51). London/New York: Rowman & Littlefield.

Lessig, L. (1999). *CODE and other laws of cyberspace.* New York: Basic Books.

Lim, M. (2012). Clicks, cabs, and coffee houses: Social media and oppositional movements in Egypt, 2004–2011. *Journal of Communication, 62,* 231–248.

Linde, H. (1972). *Sachdominanz in Sozialstrukturen.* Tübingen: Mohr.

Losey, J. (2014). The anti-counterfeiting trade agreement and European civil society: A case study on networked advocacy. *Journal of Information Policy, 4,* 205–227.

Lyon, D. (2014). Surveillance, Snowden, and big data: Capacities, consequences, critique. *Big Data & Society, July/December, 2014,* 1–13.

Mason, P. (2012). *Why it's kicking off everywhere: The new global revolutions.* London: Verso.

McAdam, D., McCarthy, J. D., & Zald, M. N. (Eds.). (1996). *Comparative perspectives on social movements: Political opportunities, mobilizing structures and cultural framings.* Cambridge: Cambridge University Press.

McAdam, D., & Scott, R. W. (2005). Organizations and movements. In G. F. Davis, D. McAdam, W. R. Scott, M. N. Zald, & N. Mayer (Eds.), *Social movements and organization theory* (pp. 4–40). Cambridge: Cambridge University Press.

McDonald, K. (2015). From Indymedia to anonymous: Rethinking action and identity in digital cultures. *Information, Communication & Society, 18*(8), 968–982.

Melucci, A. (1996). *Challenging codes. Collective action in the information age.* Cambridge: Cambridge University Press.

Milan, S. (2015). From social movements to cloud protesting: The evolution of collective identity. *Information, Communication & Society, 18*(8), 887–900.

Milkman, R., Luce, S., & Lewis, P. (2012). *Changing the subject: A bottom-up account of Occupy Wall Street in New York City.* New York: The Murphy Institute, City University of New York.

Monterde, A., Calleja-López, A., Aguilera, M., Barandiaran, X. E., & Postill, J. (2015). Multitudinous identities: A qualitative and network analysis of the 15M collective identity. *Information, Communication & Society, 18*(8), 930–950.

Morris, A. D., & Staggenborg, S. (2004). Leadership in social movements. In D. A. Snow, S. A. Soule, & H. Kriesi (Eds.), *The Blackwell companion to social movements* (pp. 171–196). Oxford: Blackwell.

Pariser, E. (2011). *The filter bubble. What the internet is hiding from you.* New York: Penguin Press.

Piven, F. F. (2013). On the organizational question. *Sociological Quarterly, 54*(2), 191–193.

Poell, T., Abdulla, R., Rieder, B., Woldering, R., & Zack, L. (2015). Protest leadership in the age of social media. *Information, Communication & Society, 19*(7), 994–1014.

Poell, T., & Van Dijck, J. (2016). Constructing public space: Global perspectives on social media and popular contestation. *International Journal of Communication, 10,* 226–234.

Popitz, H. (1992). *Phänomene der Macht.* Tübingen: Mohr Siebeck.

Rucht, D. (1984). *Modernisierung und neue soziale Bewegungen.* Frankfurt/New York: Campus.

Rucht, D. (2013). Aufstieg und Fall der Occupy-Bewegung. In K. Sonntag (Ed.), *E-Protest: Neue soziale Bewegungen und Revolutionen* (pp. 111–136). Heidelberg: Universitätsverlag Winter.

Rucht, D. (2014). Die Bedeutung von Online-Mobilisierung für Offline-Protest. In K. Voss (Ed.), *Internet und Partizipation. Bottom-up oder Top down? Politische Beteiligungsmöglichkeiten im Internet* (pp. 115–128). Wiesbaden: Springer VS.

Schrape, J.-F. (2016). *Social media, mass media and the 'public sphere.' Differentiation, complementarity and co-existence.* SOI Discussion Paper 2016-01. Stuttgart: Institute for Social Sciences.

Schulz-Schaeffer, I. (2007). *Technik als sozialer Akteur und als soziale Institution. Sozialität von Technik statt Postsozialität.* TUTS-WP-3-2007. Berlin: Technische Universität Berlin.

Simsa, R., Heinrich, M., & Totter, M. (2015). Von der Puerta del Sol ins Europaparlament. Organisationale Ausdifferenzierungen der spanischen Protestbewegung. *Forschungsjournal Soziale Bewegungen, 28*(3), 8–16.

Snow, D. A., Soule, S. A., & Kriesi, H. (Eds.). (2004a). *The Blackwell companion to social movements*. Oxford: Blackwell.

Snow, D. A., Soule, S. A., & Kriesi, H. (2004b). Mapping the terrain. In D. A. Snow, S. A. Soule, & H. Kriesi (Eds.), *The Blackwell companion to social movements* (pp. 3–16). Oxford: Blackwell.

Tilly, C., & Tarrow, S. (2015). *Contentious politics* (2nd ed.). Oxford: Oxford University Press.

Treré, E. (2012). Social movements as information ecologies: Exploring the coevolution of multiple internet technologies for activism. *International Journal of Communication, 6*, 2359–2377.

Van Dijck, J. (2013). *The culture of connectivity. A critical history of social media*. Oxford: Oxford University Press.

Van Dijck, J., & Poell, T. (2013). Understanding social media logic. *Media and Communication, 1*(1), 2–14.

Vasi, I. B., & Suh, C. S. (2016). Online activities, spatial proximity, and the diffusion of the Occupy Wall Street Movement in the United States. *Mobilization, 21*(2), 139–154.

Veg, S. (2015). Legalistic and utopian. Hong Kong's Umbrella Movement. *New Left Review, 92*, 55–73.

Yörük, E., & Yüksel, M. (2014). Class and politics in Turkey's Gezi protests. *New Left Review, 89*, 103–123.

Watkins, S. (2016). Oppositions. *New Left Review, 98*, 5–30.

Winner, L. (1980). Do artifacts have politics? *Daedalus, 109*(1), 121–136.

Chapter 4
Open Source Communities: The Sociotechnical Institutionalization of Collective Invention

Jan-Felix Schrape

Abstract Open source development has become an integral part of the software industry and a key component of the innovation strategies of all major IT providers. Against this backdrop, this article seeks to develop a systematic overview of open source communities and their socio-economic contexts. It begins with a reconstruction of the genesis of open source software projects and their changing relationships to established IT companies. This is followed by the identification of four ideal-type variants of current open source projects that differ significantly in their modes of coordination and the degree of corporate involvement. Further, the article examines why open source projects have mainly lost their subversive potential while, in contrast to former cases of collective invention, remaining viable beyond the emergence of predominant solutions and their commercial exploitation. In an industry that is characterized by very short innovation cycles, open source projects have proven to be important incubators for new product lines and branch-defining infrastructures. They do not compete against classical forms of production but instead complement and expand these.

Keywords Innovation · Open-source · Peer-production
Collective invention · Software industry · Professionalization

1 Introduction[1]

The term *open*, used in phrases from "open science" to "open innovation" and "open government," has become part of the standard vocabulary in the modern digital era (see, critically, Pomerantz and Peek 2016). Today, projects of all kinds flaunt the attribute of openness and its associated promise of more decentralized and democratic organizational and coordination structures. More specifically, the promise entails

---

[1] The research for this article was funded by the Hans-Böckler-Stiftung.

© The Author(s) 2018

U. Dolata and J.-F. Schrape, *Collectivity and Power on the Internet*,
SpringerBriefs in Sociology, https://doi.org/10.1007/978-3-319-78414-4_4

that technology could break with the traditional distribution of social roles, override established boundaries of the spheres of production and consumption and empower once-passive citizens, users, and consumers (see, for a critical overview, Dickel and Schrape 2017).

An important starting point for the popularity of the openness paradigm is the rapidly increasing relevance of open source projects in software development since the turn of the millennium. In the social sciences, accustomed to regarding intellectual property rights as primary drivers of innovation (Arrow 1962; Romer 1990), this increase was initially received with surprise (Lessig 1999). However, not long thereafter, open source became acknowledged as an emerging production model that is based on voluntary and self-directed collaboration among equals and that could reduce the significance of traditional corporations in the working world and break with well-established forms of socio-economic coordination, such as the market or hierarchy (Lakhani and von Hippel 2003). In that context, the concept of "commons-based peer production," introduced by Benkler (2002), gained traction. Hailed as a technically effective "collaboration among large groups of individuals […] without relying on either market pricing or managerial hierarchies to coordinate their common enterprise" (Benkler and Nissenbaum 2006, p. 381), commons-based peer production was to be accompanied with "systematic advantages […] in identifying and allocating human capital/creativity" (Benkler 2002, p. 381). More recently, the concept has been increasingly applied in adjacent fields, such as the production of material goods ("Maker Economy") or the service sector (e.g., Rifkin 2014, Mason 2015; Kostakis et al. 2015; Bennett and Segerberg 2015, p. 183f).

However, long-term observations of open source software (OSS) projects have shown that leading IT companies are gaining considerable influence over important projects; that the growth of the developer communities goes hand in hand with the formation of distinct hierarchical decision-making patterns; and that firmly established projects are not run by intrinsically motivated volunteers—"satisfying psychological needs, pleasure, and a sense of social belonging" (Benkler 2004, p. 1110)—but rely to a large degree on the contributions of employed developers. For example, in the Linux kernel development project, often referred to as a typical open source software project, more than 85% of the updates were made by programmers who "are being paid for their work" (Corbet and Kroah-Hartman 2016, p. 12).

Against this backdrop, this article seeks to develop a systematic overview of open source communities and their socio-economic contexts. I begin with a causal reconstruction (Mayntz 2004) of the genesis of OSS projects and their changing relationships to established IT companies on the basis of available literature, market statistics, documents and informal background talks with software engineers from Germany, Switzerland and the United States (Sect. 2). Based on aggregated empirical data, this is followed by the identification of four ideal-type variants of current OSS projects that differ from another in their modes of coordination and the degree of corporate involvement (Sect. 3). I then examine why OSS projects have mainly lost their subversive potential while, in contrast to former cases of collective invention, remaining viable beyond the emergence of predominant solutions and their commercial exploitation. Indeed, in an international software industry that is characterized by very short innovation cycles, open source projects have proven to be important incubators for new product lines and branch-defining infrastructures (Sect. 4). The final section assesses broader societal implications of the developments under discussion.

2 Reconstruction: The Genesis and Institutionalization of Open Source Projects

Soon after open source software projects became widely known, a number of books and articles were published that, offering initial explanations for their success and underlining their subversive character, essentially form the basis of the social sciences view of open source to this day (e.g., Weber 2000; Moody 2002). These texts were primarily oriented towards the narratives coming from the developer scene itself and, with few exceptions (e.g., Lerner and Tirole 2002), dispensed with any socio-economic contextualization. As the following historical reconstruction shows, however, the dividing line between free and commercial software development has never been clear-cut, and the involvement in open source projects has become an intentional, studied component of the innovation strategies of all big IT companies.

2.1 Free Software as Utopia

The development of the free software movement in the 1980s can be seen as a direct response to the previously initiated commodification of software. The first digital computers in the 1950s had been developed in close cooperation between manufacturers and users, with computer programs not yet perceived as a product that is independent from hardware but rather "as a research tool to be developed and improved by all users" (Gulley and Lakhani 2010, p. 6). Starting with the end of the 1960s, however, software began being acknowledged as a separate product. This was prompted mainly by antitrust procedures—for example, against International Business Machines (IBM), which was criticized for pushing competitors out of business with its combined offer of hardware and software (Burton 2002)—and the founding of the first specialized software companies (Fisher et al. 1983).

The spread of mini-computers (e.g., PDP-1) also played an important role in the development of a stand-alone software sector. These types of computers differed from their predecessors, the larger mainframe systems, in that their operation was much less costly, due to which they were accessible to a greater number of people and applicable to a wider range of contexts. In addition, advanced input and output interfaces (e.g., cathode ray tubes and teleprinters) engendered the development of new software genres (e.g., word processing, graphic design). At North American universities, especially, mini-computers, often donated by their manufacturers to the institutes, offered a breeding ground for the formation of informal project groups, whose members called themselves "hackers" (Levy 1984). These groups sought to overcome the limitations of existing computer systems and paved the way for the amateur computing scene that developed from the mid-1970s onward alongside the emergence of the first home computers (e.g., Altair 8800). However, the shared problem of the software architectures developed in these contexts was their *lack of legal protection*: they were published as public goods yet were hardly protected against proprietarization. For example, the Unix operating system, co-developed at universities, was commodified by AT&T from 1983 on—as soon as permitted under antitrust law (Holtgrewe and Werle 2001). Or, the computer game *Spacewar!*, programmed by students from the Massachusetts Institute of Technology (MIT) in 1961/1962, was utilized as the basis of numerous commercial video arcade machines of the 1970s and 1980s (Lowood 2009).

What commercial software providers liked less about the computer hobbyist scene was its predilection to share and circulate programs without paying or charging for them. In an open letter addressed to that community, the then-young software entrepreneur Gates (1976, p. 3) complained about this circumstance as follows:

> As the majority of hobbyists must be aware, most of you steal your software. Hardware must be paid for, but software is something to share. Who cares if the people who worked on it get paid? Is this fair? […] One thing you do is prevent good software from being written. Who can afford to do professional work for nothing? What hobbyist can put 3-man years into programming, finding all bugs, documenting his product and distribute for free? […] Most directly, the thing you do is theft.

As a result of this conflict, by the early 1980s most software products were sold solely as binary files that could not be changed and that had no accessible source code. At the same time, several amendments to copyright law in the United States increased the protection and excludability of software products (Menell 2002). As an ethical statement about this turn of events, the MIT employee Richard Stallman announced in 1983, on the then still-young Usenet, his plan to develop a free and independent operating system to go by the recursive acronym GNU ("GNU's Not Unix"):

> I consider that the golden rule requires that if I like a program I must share it with other people who like it. […] So that I can continue to use computers without violating my principles, I have decided to put together a sufficient body of free software […]. (Stallman 1983)

Although not suitable, to this day, for everyday use as a standalone operating system, the GNU project turned out to be the breeding ground for free software development. In 1985, Stallman established the Free Software Foundation (FSF), which, starting with 1988, enlisted the first large-scale industrial sponsors such as the hardware manufacturers Sony and Hewlett-Packard, who had an interest in inexpensively licensable software. The most important innovation, however, was the *introduction of robust licensing models*, like the General Public License (GPL) published in 1989, which legally ensure that any forks of the free software remain free:

> Each time you redistribute the Program (or any work based on the Program), the recipient automatically receives a license from the original licensor to copy, distribute or modify the Pro-gram subject to these terms and conditions. You may not impose any further restrictions on the recipients' exercise of the rights granted herein. (Free Software Foundation 1989)

From 2001 on, violations of the GPL were the object of numerous court proceedings against companies such as Skype, Cisco and D-Link (Stiller 2011; Jaeger 2010). It should be noted, however, that "the court of public opinion" played an equally important role in the Usenet, and later on the World Wide Web, for the establishment of the reciprocity principles in the GPL (O'Mahony 2003, p. 1189).

That said, the success of the GNU project remained limited at first due to its reliance on costly workstations and its strong ideological connotations—two problems to which the Linux kernel development project offered a solution. Linux was introduced in 1991 by then-student Linus Torvalds as a free operating system kernel for the more affordable micro-computers, which made it attractive and accessible for a larger number of developers. In addition, the Linux kernel project, or rather its founder, was characterized from the start by a much more liberal attitude than the Free Software Foundation: "This world would be a much better place if people had less ideology and a whole lot more 'I do this because it's fun and because others might find it useful, not because I got religion'" (Torvalds 2002). Another reason for the success of Linux was the spread of the World Wide Web from 1993 on, as that facilitated both access to and participation in the project and its coordination.

Nonetheless, the Linux kernel project was initially known only within expert circles. Indeed, it was not until the publication of the widely read book *The Cathedral and the Bazaar* in 1999, already presented as an essay by software developer Eric S. Raymond in 1997, that the Linux kernel became more widely known. The main thesis of the book was: Whereas in traditional production models a program's source code is only published for the final version, with developer groups being hierarchically organized—corresponding to the *cathedral*—the source code in projects like the Linux Kernel or Fetchmail (then coordinated by Raymond) is always visible and their developer groups are horizontally structured as well as maintained by modular self-organization without central management—corresponding to a *bazaar*. Nonetheless, critical observers observed early on that while in both cases (Linux Kernel, Fetchmail) many suggestions came from the project community, the final changes were released by only one person, being either Torvalds or Raymond (Connell 2000; Bezroukov 1999a, b). In other words:

> The only entity that can really succeed in developing Linux is the entity that is trusted to do the right thing. And as it stands right now, I'm the only person/entity that has that degree of trust. And even if somebody thought I was doing a bad job (which is fairly rare) and that somebody decides that "I really want to fix this feature," there's a really big hurdle to convince everybody else that he CAN fix that feature. (Torvalds 1998, p. 36)

Overall, GNU and Linux stand as two main flagship projects for free software development of the 1980s and 1990s whose success was greatly facilitated by the increased efficiency of communication brought about by the internet. This environment spurred the emergence of legal instruments such as the General Public License (GPL), which protect collective work results from being claimed or appropriated by any one individual or entity. It was in this context that the first narratives circulated that hailed free software development as the new and upcoming way to produce software without asymmetries of power. These narratives gained, at least for some time, currency among social scientists (e.g., Benkler 2002; Tapscott and Williams 2006), although informed observers identified them early on as rather biased descriptions of the "hacker culture" (e.g., Bezroukov 1999b).

2.2   Open Source as Method

In the subsequent decade of the 2000s, open source became an increasingly recognized working method within the software industry. Apart from the continuing spread of the internet, this may be attributed to the following dynamics.

First, a growing number of companies began outsourcing the development of software products to the open source field. Of those, Netscape Communications was a rather conspicuous, and early, case in point. When it became evident that Microsoft would be crowding out Netscape Navigator with its Windows-integrated Internet Explorer, Netscape announced in 1998 that it would transfer large portions of its web browser code to the open source *Mozilla project*. This project, which engendered the popular web browser Firefox in 2004, received financial and human resources support from AOL/Netscape until the founding of the Mozilla Foundation in 2003. With its 1998 announcement, Netscape aimed primarily to build and diversify its clientele: "By making our source code available to the internet community, Netscape can expand its client software leadership by […] building a community that addresses markets and needs we can't address on our own […]."

Secondly, at the beginning of 1998, a developer group that had formed around Eric S. Raymond concluded that the term "free software" could impede the spread of software with a GPL or similar license in commercial contexts given its political connotations. They therefore introduced the *new label "open source,"* which they considered to emphasize the superiority of this development model while deflecting from any socio-political aspects (Raymond 1998). As part of that process, they also founded the Open Source Initiative, namely with the help of protagonists such as Tim O'Reilly, who was to later coin the term "Web 2.0." However, to this day, this change of course has not been endorsed by the Free Software Foundation: "For the Open Source movement, non-free software is a suboptimal solution. For the Free Software movement, non-free software is a social problem and free software is the solution" (Stallman 2002, p. 57). This disagreement was representative of the fundamental divide that had been fermenting and that, ongoing to this day, some try to evade by means of hybrid acronyms such as FLOSS (Free/Libre Open Source Software) or FOSS (Free & Open Source Software).

The *third* main factor that contributed to the recognition of open source as a working method was the *stock market success* of some open source companies in 1999 as a result of the dot-com boom of the late 1990s. Among these companies

Table 1 The most commonly used open source licenses worldwide

	E.g., used by	2018 (%)	2010 (%)	Orientation	Publication
GNU Public License 2.0	Linux kernel, WordPress	18	47	Strongly protective	1991
MIT License	jQuery, Ruby on Rails	32	6	Permissive	1988
Apache License 2.0	Android, Apache HTTP Server	14	4	Permissive	2004
GNU Public License 3.0	GNU Compiler Collection	7	6	Strongly protective	2007
BSD License 2.0 (3-clause)	Chromium, WebKit	6	6	Permissive	1999
Artistic License 1/2	Perl	4	9	Permissive	2000/2006
GNU Lesser GPL 2.1/3.0	VLC Media Player	6	9	Weakly protective	1999/2007
Microsoft Public License	Microsoft Azure	1	2	Permissive	2007
Eclipse Public License	Eclipse	1	1	Permissive	2004

Source Black Duck Knowledgebase (Status: 1/2018)

were the Linux-oriented hardware vendors VA Linux and Cobalt Networks as well as the software provider Red Hat, which specialized in Linux software architectures for enterprises. The initial public offerings (IPOs) of these three companies were, in fact, among the most spectacular of all time, resulting in mass media attention for the open source scene as a whole (e.g., Gelsi 1999).

These interrelated trends and processes, combined with the continued expansion of the IT market, led to the rapid proliferation of open source projects. Indeed, the number of projects grew from only several hundred in 1999 to the several million projects which can today be found on platforms such as GitHub and SourceForge. Given this dramatic increase in the number of projects, accompanied by novel licensing models created by companies and foundations, open source licensing has also been subject to very strong diversification (Table 1). Alongside original "copyleft" licenses such as the General Public License (GPL), which guarantee that free software must be forked under the same conditions (*strongly protective*), additional licenses have been issued that permit the inclusion of free software in proprietary products as long as these elements remain open source (*weakly protective*) or even permit the publication of subsequent derivations or branches under downright restrictive conditions (*permissive*). This diversity greatly expands the strategic options, especially for commercial stakeholders (Lerner and Schankerman 2010; Lerner and Tirole 2005). After the GPL 3.0 was published, closing previous gaps, Apple replaced the GNU compiler collection (GCC) in its development environment Xcode with a solution with a permissive licence; Google decided from the outset to put project's own code of Android under the Apache 2.0 License.

Concurrently, we can observe a corporatization of open source projects in two ways. On the one hand, branch-defining development projects such as the Linux kernel, the Apache HTTP Server and the cloud computing architecture OpenStack are today funded primarily by donations from companies or operate like the browser engine WebKit (Apple) and the mobile operating system Android (Google) under the aegis of commercial providers (Fitzgerald 2006). On the other hand, the developer base of large-scale projects is increasingly financed by business circles. According to Kolassa et al. (2014), in the Linux kernel and 5000 other market-relevant projects, more than 50% of all contributions that occurred between 2000 and 2011 were made during standard 9-to-5 working hours. The Linux Foundation, for its part, observed that the portion of independent programmers in kernel development (2009: 18%, 2014: 12%, 2016: 8%) is steadily declining compared to that of company-associated contributors (Table 2).

It is in this way that open source development increasingly became enmeshed with the software industry over the past two decades—albeit not without losing, to a large extent, its initial force as a counterbalance to proprietary production.[2] Overall, apart from smaller projects (such as the Linux distributions Arch or Parabola) that are still true to the original maxims of free software, most open source projects today involve the participation of established IT companies. The latter use these working environments as a means to protect standards that are favorable to them and to expand their internal proprietary and undisclosed development activities through "controlled openings at the edges" (Dolata 2017, p. 20). In this respect, the blogger Bulajewski (2011) finds, rightly so, the image of open source projects as communities "of volunteer programmers collaborating together in a gift economy" to be an illusion.

2.3 Open Source as Innovation Strategy

In particular in the enterprise software markets, which account for more than 80% of global software sales, "a widespread use of open-source technology" can now be observed (Driver 2014; Miller and Nelson 2016). In addition, open source solutions are predominating in the area of basic IT infrastructures such as web servers and content management systems (Table 3). Market researchers attribute this not only to the cost advantages but also to the adaptability and "inherent trialability" of open source solutions (Spinellis and Giannikas 2012, p. 667). As a result, it is not surprising that today most major IT companies (Table 4) are involved in open source projects.

Microsoft—the company, which has long termed open source as an "intellectual property destroyer" (Hayes 2001, p. 78)—launched its subsidiary MS Open Technologies in 2012. Since then, it has put the .NET Framework, software development kits for its cloud computing service Azure as well as many other components under

---

[2]Under the label "inner sourcing" (O'Reilly 2000), an increasing number of firms are adapting the development methods of OSS projects for their internal coordination structures; however, agile methods had been in use in the IT industry as early as the 1990s (Martin 1991).

Table 2 Contributions to the Linux kernel (changes, in %) *Korporative Akteure*

	2016–2017 (R. 4.8–4.13) [%]	2015–2016 (R 3.19–4.7) [%]	2013–2014 (R 3.11–3.18) [%]	2011–2013 (R 3.0–3.10) [%]	2010–2012 (R 2.6.36–3.2) [%]	2005–2009 (R 2.6.1–3.6.3) [%]
Independent	8.2	7.7	12.4	13.6	16.2	18.2
Unknown	4.1	6.8	4.9	3.3	4.3	7.6
Intel	13.1	12.9	10.5	8.8	7.2	5.3
Red Hat	7.2	8.0	8.4	10.2	10.7	12.3
Linaro	5.6	4.0	5.6	4.1	0.7	n.a.
Samsung	3.2	3.9	4.4	2.6	1.7	n.a.
IBM	4.1	2.7	3.2	3.1	3.7	7.6
SUSE	3.0	3.2	3.0	3.5	4.3	7.6
Consultants	3.3	2.6	2.5	1.7	2.6	2.5
Texas Instruments	1.4	1.7	2.4	4.1	3.0	n.a.
Vision Engraving	n.a.	1.3	2.2	2.3	n.a.	n.a.
Google	3.0	2.0	2.1	2.4	1.5	0.9
Other companies	43.8	43.2	38.4	40.3	44.8	38.0
Intel, Red Hat, Samsung, IBM combined	27.6	27.5	26.5	24.7	23.3	25.2

Sources Corbet et al. (2009–2015), Corbet and Kroah-Hartman (2016, 2017)

Table 3 Estimated global market share of OSS (in %, installed base/usage share)

	Open source	2010	2017	Competitors	2010	2017
Operating system personal computer[a]	GNU/Linux	1	2	MS Windows	94	89
				Apple Mac OS X	5	9
Operating system mobile devices[b]	Android	11	69	Apple iOS	30	28
				Symbian/Nokia OS	33	>0.5
					–	>0.5
				Windows Phone	14	>0.5
				Blackberry		
Web browser [desktop][c]	Mozilla Firefox	31	13	MS IE (+Edge)	47	13
	Google Chrome*	14	64	Apple Safari	5	6
Operating system public servers[d]	Linux (incl. Unix-like)	69	67	MS Windows	31	33
Web server [active sites][e]	Apache	72	48	Microsoft IIS	21	10
	Nginx	4	37	Google Servers	1	1
Web content management system[f]	WordPress	51	60	Blogger (Google)	2	2
	Joomla	12	6	Bitrix	–	1
	Drupal	7	5	vBulletin	8	>0.5

Sources [a, b]NetApplications; [c]StatCounter; [d–f]W3techs (Status: 1/2018)
*Mainly based on the Chromium OSS project

Table 4 Largest public internet, IT and software companies (May 2017)

	Sales In billion US$ (FY)	Market cap In billion US$	Employees
Apple	217	752	116,000
Samsung Electronics	174	254	93,200
Amazon.com	136	427	341,400
Alphabet (Google)	90	579	72,053
Microsoft	85	507	114,000
IBM	80	162	380,000
HP Inc.	49	29	49,000
Oracle	37	182	136,000
Facebook	28	407	17,048
SAP	24	120	84,183

Sources Forbes 2000 (Status: 1/2018)

a free license, namely in order "to achieve a strategic objective, such as promoting industry standards, advancing interoperability, or attracting and enabling our external development community" (Microsoft 2017, p. 20). It would be difficult to estimate what proportion of leading software companies' R&D budgets goes to open source projects since the integration of open source elements is now standard practice in numerous manufacturer-specific architectures. *Apple*'s operating system packages macOS, iOS, tvOS and watchOS, for example, are in its core based on the Unix-like operating system Darwin and contain hundreds of other OSS components, such as WebKit (browser engine), CUPS (printing system) and XQuartz (Window System).

At the turn of the millennium, *IBM* had already invested several hundred million US dollars in the development of Linux, namely as a means to counteract Microsoft's dominance in the enterprise sector and to set up a service business around open source software. Today, IBM is involved in well over 100 open source projects, among them the cloud computing platform OpenStack, in which *Intel* and *Hewlett-Packard* also participate. However, that involvement results less from idealism than from pragmatic strategizing: "Such actions are comparable to giving away the razor (the code) to sell more razor blades (the related consulting services that IBM and HP hope to provide)" (Lerner 2012, p. 43). It is for similar reasons that SAP, Oracle and Adobe are participating in open source projects. In addition, many consumer electronics products from Samsung and other leading companies—such as TVs, tablets, phones and cameras—are enabled with open source software. For smaller IT providers, in particular, an involvement in open source projects also serves as a "marketing tool to increase brand recognition" (Dahlander and Magnusson 2008, p. 638).

A special variant of corporate open source exposures is the development of the Android operating system for mobile devices by the Open Handset Alliance, initiated and led by *Google*. Advertised as a pure open source project and often presented in the literature along the same lines as projects such as the Linux kernel (e.g., Herstatt and Ehls 2015, p. XVII), the development of the operating system is de facto controlled by Google alone. The Android code is run under permissive licenses, which, in combination with further frameworks such as the "Compatibility Definition Document" (CDD), essentially gives Google comprehensive steering control. "Because it fully controls the development of the OS, Google can determine the technological specifications to which Android partners must abide" (Spreeuwenberg and Poell 2012). With the launch of Android, Google apparently succeeded above all in facilitating the seamless access to its own services and offers for as many IT devices as possible. For example, whereas Google generated approximately 99% of its revenue from advertising in 2007, the sale of its digital content and services accounted for 11% of sales (US$90 billion) in 2016 (Alphabet 2016).

In addition, the end of the 1990s saw the emergence of a number of "open source companies," which were giving away their core product—the software code—free of charge while endeavoring to build a business through support services. However, with the exception of the Linux distributor Red Hat, which had been cooperating early on with leading hardware vendors and which today is market leader in enterprise Linux systems, most of the companies that were launched during the dot-com boom quickly folded (Ante 2014; Levine 2014). And although the open source environment has

Table 5 Popular projects on Open Hub (web catalog for open-source projects)

Project	Commits (last year)[a]	Umbrella organization	Primary funding source
Android	104,151	Google Inc., Open Handset Alliance (84+ companies)	
KDE	87,466	KDE e.V.	Patronages (includes Google, SUSE, Qt)
Chromium	77,562	Google Inc.	
OpenStack	76,130	OpenStack Foundation	Members (includes HP, IBM, Red Hat)
Linux Kernel	73,254	Linux Foundation	Members (includes HP, Intel, IBM, Red Hat)
Mozilla Firefox	53,255	Mozilla Foundation	Donations, royalties (until 2014: 90% Google)
Ubuntu (Touch)	52,128[b]	Canonical Ltd.	Canonical, partners (includes Intel, Cisco, HP)
Fedora	34,222	Fedora Project (Red Hat)	Red Hat Inc.
Debian Linux	26,782	Debian Project	Donations, partners (includes HP, 1&1)
LibreOffice	15,733	Document Foundation	Donations (includes Google, Red Hat, Intel)
WebKit	13,059	Apple Inc.	
Eclipse IDE	7715	Eclipse Foundation	Members (includes IBM, SAP, Oracle, Bosch)
GNU CC	7602	Free Software Foundation	Members, patronages (includes Google, IBM)
OpenSSL	3225	– (OpenSSL Foundation)	Since 2014: Core Infrastructure Initiative
Joomla!	2884	Open Source Matters NPO	Sponsors, advertising, affiliates
WordPress	2348	WordPress Foundation	Automattic Inc., donations, events
Apache HTTP	2103	Apache Foundation	Donations (includes Google, Microsoft)
Arch Linux	252	–	Smaller private donations
jEdit	178	–	Smaller private donations

Sources Open Hub (5/2017); Annual Reports; [a]Updates 1/2016–1/2017; [b]2015–2016

recently given rise to new start-ups such as Hortonworks (launched in 2011) most of these companies do not even emphasize "open source" in their self-presentation and are characterized by a low level of identification with Stallman's ideals of reciprocity:

> There is a tension between the GPL [GNU General Public License] and business which has consequences for what we can do and what we want to do. At the end of the day, the company must earn money to survive. Richard Stallman has a very idealistic view of the world, which is admirable. But if one considers it from a business perspective one realizes that it is not feasible in practice. (Open source service platform provider, in Bergquist et al. 2012, p. 8)

Indeed, today it is, in contrast, mainly established corporations such as IBM ("Open Source & Standards are key to making our planet smarter") or Microsoft ("Openness builds bridges between platforms and people") that are referring to certain selected maxims of free software in their public relations.

In that sense, many of today's popular open source communities have close financial ties with leading IT companies, which are deliberately investing in open source projects as part of their overarching innovation strategies (Table 5).[3] In the case of corporate-initiated projects (such as Android or OpenStack), this entanglement is obvious. However, even foundation-supported communities (such as the Apache HTTP Server or GNU) grant their donors seats on the boards of their umbrella organizations. The latter, while not directly in control of the development activities, provide the technical infrastructures and distribute financial resources. Together with their involvement in the code development as such, these leading IT companies are thereby securing a considerable influence on relevant development projects while at the same time allowing for greater predictability in the planning of these projects as regards both their human and financial resources.

3 Typology: Varieties of Open Source Software Projects

Over the last 20 years, OSS has thus become an integral part of the IT industry. Against this background, the array of open source projects has become larger and broader. At one end of the spectrum, some communities are still committed to Stallman's socio-ethical ideals, operate independently of corporate interests, and are largely aligned with egalitarian organizational principles. At the other end of the spectrum, we find a large number of projects that are under the direct control of leading IT companies and that follow hierarchical development models. From an organizational-sociological point of view (i.a. van de Ven et al. 1976; Scott 2004; Ahrne et al. 2016) and based on available empirical data (e.g., licensing documents, certificates, technical specifications, membership listings, mailing lists, wikis), four ideal-type variants of recent

---

[3]For instance, a significant part of Mozilla's income arrives in the form of royalties from the Firefox search box, in other words, contracts with major search engine providers. The main sponsors of the Apache Software Foundation include Google, Microsoft and Facebook as platinum members with donations of $100,000+ per year.

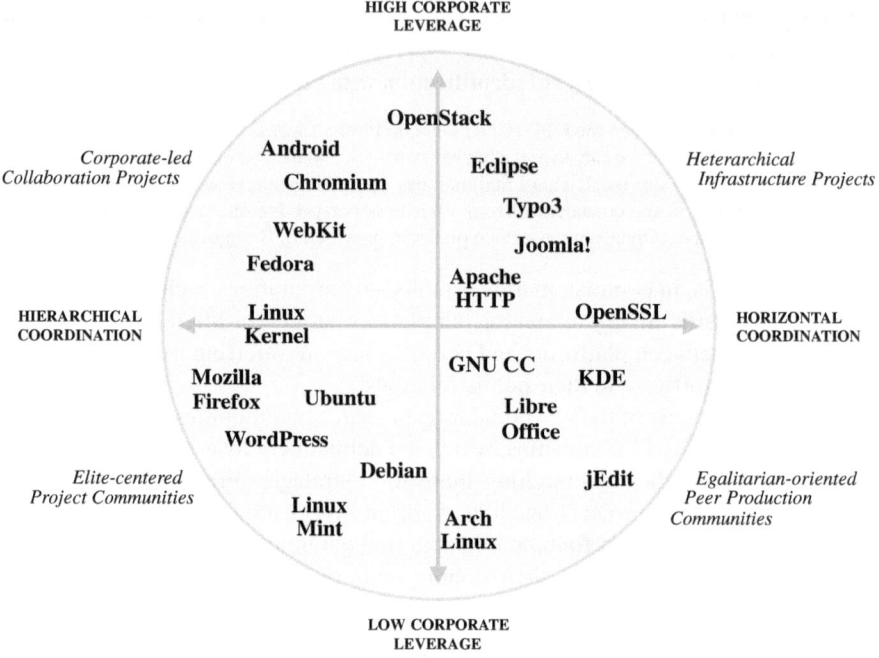

Fig. 1 Varieties of OSS projects

open-source projects can be distinguished according to their prevailing forms of coordination and degree of corporate involvement (Fig. 1).

Corporate-led collaboration projects are characterized by clear work hierarchies and a strong market presence of its products. Their communities are composed primarily of programmers who are employed by the participating companies. In Android, WebKit (rendering engine for web browser) and Fedora (Linux distribution), the strategic control clearly lies with Google, Apple or Red Hat, respectively. In the cloud computing project OpenStack, big sponsors (e.g., Rackspace, Intel, IBM, Red Hat, AT&T, Deutsche Telekom, Cisco) likewise have considerable influence: "This new kind of community […] is clearly driven by corporate interests. Participating companies, which may be commercial competitors, have clear strategies towards the project […]" (Gonzalez-Barahona et al. 2013, p. 39).

Moreover, when this type of corporate collaboration takes place under the terms of OSS projects, it allows to overcome two classic knowledge-sharing dilemmas (Larsson et al. 1998; Cabrera and Cabrera 2002): One, open source licenses prevent the proprietarization of the collectively developed code by any individual entity and, secondly, these same licenses prevent abuse from free riders given the traceability of which companies use which elements and of whether they participated in the development (Henkel et al. 2014; Sydow et al. 2016, pp. 233–252). In addition, in this day and age, it is often easier to create new software products by building on already existing open source elements than by developing the software from scratch (West and Bogers 2014, 2017).

Heterarchical infrastructure projects, whose products are ever-present beneath the visible surface of IT architectures, are closely intertwined with corporate contexts. Some were initially based (like the integrated development environment Eclipse) on architectures that were formerly proprietary. Others were (like the Apache HTTP Server) characterized by rapid organic growth in their beginnings, since they offered solutions to previously unaddressed challenges, making them interesting to companies early on, especially as open infrastructures do not carry an impetus for application code or hardware to be open itself (Weinberg 2015a; Greenstein and Nagle 2014).[4] Today, infrastructure projects are primarily supported by medium and large IT companies; however, their communities are not guided by corporate core circles but mostly operate under the umbrella of nonprofit organizations or foundations and are structured horizontally along working groups. Management positions are assigned on a meritocratic basis ("the more you contribute, the more responsibility you will earn"). But in these projects, too, employed developers, who are explicitly freed from other tasks by their companies to work in the community, are more likely than leisure or lay programmers to advance to decision-making positions.

An infrastructure project that points to the potential risks of the open source model is the encryption software OpenSSL, which is used in many operating systems and platforms since the 1990s: Until 2014, OpenSSL was developed by one sole full-time programmer who was assisted by a very small, voluntary team and received little financial support from the industry. In that context, ever new features were integrated into OpenSSL—yet without bolstering the level of maintenance work accordingly. In 2012, then, this culminated in an oversight that led to the major "Heartbleed" vulnerability, which was not discovered until 2014 (Stokel-Walker 2014; Perlroth 2014). In light of this "worst vulnerability found [...] since commercial traffic began to flow on the Internet" (Steinberg 2014), the Linux Foundation and leading companies formed the Core Infrastructure Initiative to fund projects that are critical to the functioning of the web.

Elite-centric project communities are likewise based largely on the contributions of developers who are affiliated with companies, but these contributors are not under the direct control of a commercial actor. Rather, their coordination takes place along differentiated decision-making pyramids, or a "lieutenant system built around a chain of trust" (Kernel.Org 2016) that is headed by an elected project manager (e.g., Debian Linux), a management team (e.g., Mozilla) or its founder as a "benevolent dictator." Linus Torvalds, for instance, "is the final arbiter of all changes accepted into the Linux kernel" (Kernel.Org 2016) and Mark Shuttleworth as "self-appointed benevolent dictator for life [...] plays a happily undemocratic role" as sponsor of the Ubuntu project (Ubuntu 2017). That said, neither Torvalds nor Shuttleworth would be well advised to regularly override the decisions of the technical boards, provided that they

---

[4]As Weinberg (2015b) notes, the mobile operation system Android therefore "provides an apt analogy. While the platform derives from hundreds of open source components [...], the majority of the applications distributed through Google Play are closed and proprietary."

would like to see strong community involvement in the long run. And with the launch of Firefox, Mozilla also installed a "rather rigorously controlled model" (Stamelos 2014, p. 328)—from "super-reviewers" and "stewards" to two "ultimate decision makers."[5]

While such a top-down management curtails the leverage of the participants, it also counteracts fragmentation (Coleman 2013; Snow 2014; O'Mahony and Ferraro 2007). In that sense, Linux Mint initiator Clement Lefebvre (in Byfield 2013) states: "The final decision comes from the top [...]. Strong leadership is important and benefits Linux Mint, [because] the decisions we take remain consistent and are coherent with our overall vision." In Debian or Mozilla, the project guidelines are formally fixed; in the Linux kernel project, by contrast, Torvald's leadership style gave rise to "opaque governing norms" that risk counteracting the openness of the project in the event of a conflict. According to Kreiss, Finn and Turner "[...] without the law or a clear mechanism of accountability those injured by or excluded from peer production processes have very limited recourse. The only alternative for these individuals is to not participate" (2011, p. 252).

Egalitarian-oriented peer production communities are in turn, based on their self-understanding, about market-independent, intrinsic and equitable collaboration among volunteers. "Basically, people who participate in peer production communities love it. They feel passionate about their particular area of expertise and revel in creating something new or better" (Tapscott and Williams 2006, p. 70). However, as is apparent from KDE (a community for desktop environments), GNU or LibreOffice, once these communities reach a certain size, they usually feature more classical leadership structures and a stable roster of corporate stakeholders. For instance, the KDE project does not have one single project manager but instead the "KDE Core Team" consisting of several dozen contributors who decide on the overall direction of the KDE platform (KDE 2017); the GNU Compiler Collection is managed by the "GCC steering committee [...] with the intent of preventing any particular individual, group or organization from getting control over the project" (GNU 2017).

By contrast, intrinsically motivated communities such as Arch (Linux distribution) or jEdit (text editor) target their products to very specific user groups, are rather irrelevant to the general market and are run by small teams, due to which they have so far been able to do without pronounced social structures or membership rules ("You can 'join' simply by subscribing to the [...] mailing lists"). Still, even smaller developer communities are marked by technical and social contribution barriers, "including steep learning curve, lack of community support, and difficulties finding out how to start" (Steinmacher et al. 2015, p. 1380); and when such communities grow, alongside the intensity of their interactions with external market actors, they too tend

---

[5]Since 1998, former Netscape manager Mitchell Baker holds one of these positions and is also executive chairwoman of the Mozilla Cooperation and the Foundation, which has over 1000 employees. Although voluntary participants are welcomed, between September 2015 and September 2016, only 17 volunteers but 228 new hires were introduced in the project's weekly updates (Mozilla 2016). The Ubuntu project, too, relies on the work of the employees of Shuttleworth's for-profit company Canonical.

Table 6 Ideal-type manifestations of open source projects

	Corporate-led collaboration projects	Elite-centered project communities	Heterarchical infrastructure projects	Egalitarian-oriented peer production communities
	E.g., *Android, WebKit, OpenStack*	E.g., *Linux Kernel, Firefox, Ubuntu*	E.g., *Apache HTTP, Eclipse, Joomla!*	E.g., *GNU CC, Arch Linux, KDE*
Work organization	Mainly hierarchical	Mainly hierarchical	Horizontal—meritocratic	Horizontal—egalitarian
Strategic management	Individual companies/consortium of firms	Project founder/long-term project management team	Board of directors of the foundation/Steering group	Steering committee/core team
Funding	Participating companies	Corporate donations/smaller private donations	Primarily contributions from companies	Primarily smaller private donations
Participant pool	Mainly staff from the participating companies	Employed and (few) voluntary developers	Employed developers, and explicit company representatives	Primarily voluntary developers Entwickler

to adopt "cathedral-like" organizational modes, regardless of the level of technical efficiency they may have attained.

The common denominator of all four project variants is their underlying open source licensing models, which protect their products from direct proprietarization. Nonetheless, the "rebel code" spirit (Moody 2002) of these projects has, at this point, been significantly diluted. Despite the enhanced technological possibilities for coordination, all larger open source projects give rise to hierarchical decision-making routines as well as distinct management circles and tend to become enmeshed in market contexts if they operate in the long term and are able to reach larger target groups or to provide comprehensively used IT infrastructures (Table 6). Contrary to the notion that "organizations [...] really don't matter as much as they used to" (Suddaby 2013, p. 1009), conventional companies and non-for-profits are not losing their influence over open source projects and are instead maintaining their status and role as the initiators and central funders of many open collaboration projects in the software industry.

4   Discussion: The Sociotechnical Institutionalization of Collective Invention

The preceding chapters debunk two long-prevailing assumptions. One, that the technical infrastructures of the internet, seen to promote decentralized working methods and to offer "easier pathways to challenge oligarchy," can, on their own, effectively resist an "ossification of power" in OSS projects (Benkler 2013, p. 225). And two, that there is a "networked information economy" (Benkler 2006, p. 3) in which corporate actors (companies, non-governmental organizations, research institutes) suffer a loss of their relevance in the face of "nonproprietary, voluntaristic, self-assisted practices" (Benkler 2013, p. 213). These assumptions do not hold for two main reasons.

First, although the infrastructures and services used in open source projects lay the foundation for the work processes and the optimized coordination of tasks, they in no way lead to a disintermediation or loss of relevance of *social structuring patterns*. In other words, in open source communities and similar web-based communities (such as Wikipedia), too, collectively accepted rules, guidelines and hierarchical decision-making structures emerge that are characterized by strong power asymmetries. Indeed, such social institutionalization dynamics are a fundamental prerequisite for an open source project to be perceived as an entity (by the project developers themselves as well as by external actors), to be capable of intentional and strategic action, and to gain broader momentum (Dobusch et al. 2017; Dolata and Schrape 2016; O'Mahony and Ferraro 2007).

Secondly, corporate players usually have more leverage than communities of interest to act systematically and reliably, namely because they have *formalized decision-making routines* as well as the discretion to utilize their resources regardless of their members' preferences (see, e.g., Perrow 1991; Blau and Scott 1962). In addition, companies and other organizations are able to bring in their resources more continuously and consistently than individual contributors. As a result, for-profit and not-for-profit organizations significantly contribute to creating a reliable, predictable planning environment for open source projects, in turn garnering them considerable clout and influence over the community. Moreover, independent projects are often linked to associated non-profit organizations that offer them an umbrella identity and that stabilize the community in the event of conflicts (Ahrne et al. 2016).

In that context, open source projects could be seen to be subject not only to corporatization but also to a steadily intensifying embracement by established market actors. Indeed, the reconstruction of the history of OSS development presented above shows that the commonly portrayed ideal image of an independent commons-based peer production existed primarily in the early days of free software. However, as early as the end of the 1990s, the then internet-focused start-up scene relied heavily on inexpensively licensed open source components, followed by, starting with the turn of the millennium, the increasing involvement of other companies in open source projects—IBM being an early case in point. From the point of view of innovation research, such a development does not necessarily seem unusual: Like other (radical) niche innovations, free software projects were initially "carried and developed by small networks of dedicated actors, often outsiders or fringe actors," yet became subject to a professionalization and appropriation on the part of established economic actors as soon as they caught the attention of the mainstream markets (Geels and Schot 2007, p. 400; Dolata 2013, p. 68).

History has seen many episodes of collective invention (Table 7) during which corporate or individual actors openly shared their knowledge in niches decoupled from the general market, thereby benefiting from "cumulative advance" (Allen 1983; Powell and Giannella 2010; Lamoreaux and Sokoloff 2000; Scranton 1997):

> To the degree that economists have considered this behaviour at all, it has been regarded as an undesired "leakage" that reduces the incentives to invent. That firms desire such behaviour and that it increases the rate of invention […] are possibilities not yet explored. (Allen 1983, p. 21)

However, in sharp contrast to former cases of collective invention, OSS projects remain viable beyond the initial stages of the innovation process and beyond the emergence of predominant solutions and their commercial exploitation (Osterloh and Rota 2007). This may be attributed to the following interacting factors:

- Early on in its development, the free software scene gave rise to informal rules as well as *novel licensing models* designed to prevent the proprietarization and commodification of collective work results. Today, these models comprise the core framework of OSS projects, allowing for a reliable project-specific collaboration and exchange of knowledge between individual developers as well as companies that may be direct competitors otherwise (e.g., Apple and Samsung).
- At the same time, the *rapid advance of online technologies* has allowed for much greater efficiency in the verification of compliance with these licensing conditions and has facilitated not only the access to projects but also the spread and use of their products. In addition, it has contributed to solving a long-term problem faced

Table 7 Some historical episodes of collective invention

Episode	Knowledge exchange	Outcome
The Cornish Pumping Engine Approx. 1810–1850, Cornwall, England	Exchange of technical know-how; comparison of progress via journals	Development of an efficient steaming engine for the mining industry
Paper manufacture Approx. 1827–1857, New England, USA	Stable community of mill owners; regular informal exchange of experiences	Increase in productivity by mechanization of the entire production process
Furnace technologies Approx. 1850–1880, Cleveland Dis., England	Exchange of knowledge via journals; collective trial-and-error process	Reduction of energy demand by height and temperature adjustments
Flat-panel displays Approx. 1969–1989, Japan/Europe/USA	Publication of proprietary research results in technical journals	Incremental development in the pre-commercial phase
Homebrew Computer Club Approx. 1975–1978 [1986], San Francisco Bay area, USA	Free exchange until the success of participating firms (e.g., Apple Inc.)	Development of the first personal computers for the mass market

Sources Allen (1983), McGaw (1987), Spencer (2003), Meyer (2003), Nuvolari (2004)

by the software sector, namely that of coordinating large projects with developers working in different contexts and from different geographical locations (Brooks 1975; Campbell-Kelly 2003).

- Finally, and most importantly, in an international software industry that has been expanding for decades[6] and that is characterized by very short innovation cycles, open source projects have proven to be pivotal *incubators for branch-defining infrastructures*, standards and platforms (such as the Apache HTTP Server, the Linux kernel, or OpenStack). This applies all the more since OSS can be tested by the developers themselves and adapted to their respective requirements with little administrative effort (Spinellis and Giannikas 2012).

From the 1980s on, the ongoing success of open source projects was determined by the expansion of digital connectivity, the establishment of widely accepted informal rules and conventions for work and practice and, last but not least, the creation of reliable licensing models. Strongly protective "copyleft" licenses (e.g., the GNU General Public License) and their derivatives (e.g., permissive licenses such as the MIT License or the Apache License 2.0), aided by the online technologies, have contributed to ensuring the longevity of collective invention through sociotechnical means. Thus, at the turn of the millennium, a novel form of collaboration that initially took place in subversive niches was adapted into a supplementary working method by the commercial software industry and is today a key element of the innovation strategies of all established IT providers (Fig. 2).

---

[6]Worldwide spending for software and IT services 2005: US$885 billion; 2010: US$1,092 billion; 2015: US$1,532 billion (UNCTAD 2012; Accelerance 2017).

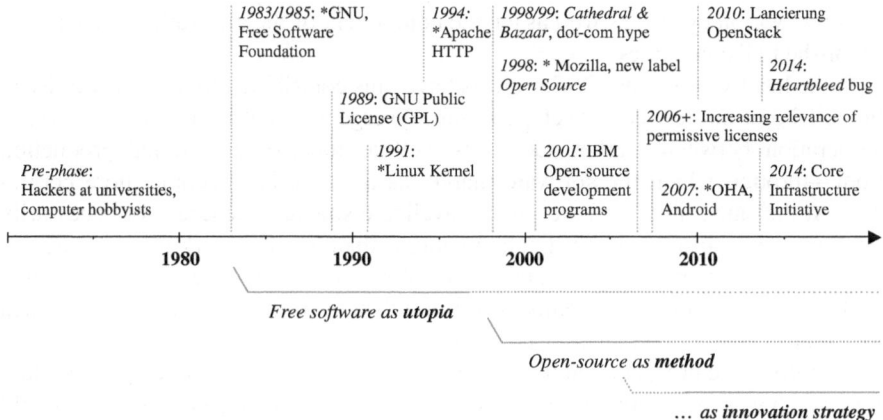

Fig. 2 Open source as utopia, method and innovation strategy

In that sense, open source licensing models no longer can be seen as a "form of institutional jiujitsu" (Benkler 2002, p. 446) that aims for the total dissolution of intellectual property rights (for an incisive critical overview, see Coleman 2013, pp. 185–215). Instead, these licenses comprise the legal and structural basis of collaboration projects that, as incubators of innovation, do not compete against established forms of socio-economic production but instead complement and expand these (Allen and Potts 2016). Since open source software (and hardware) projects have proven to be more than just a flash in the pan, it may be worthwhile to recognize them as fourth enduring source of invention and technological change (see Jewkes et al. 1969; Allen 1983)—in addition to individual inventors, not-for-profit organizations (e.g., universities, public research centers), and the R&D departments of private firms.

5 Conclusions

Overall, the relationship between the task-oriented working structures of open source projects and the established forms of economic coordination (e.g., market, hierarchy) is not characterized by competition but by complementariness. While OSS projects have largely lost their formatting as a counterpart to commercial production, they have, unlike previous types of collective invention, remained viable beyond the initial phase of innovation processes. Open source licenses, together with the coordination-facilitating features of the online technologies, have established the sociotechnical framework for a permanent form of open and collaborative development. Initially, this framework was applied in subversive niches and later adapted by the commercial software industry as a complementary software development method. Today, open source projects have become important incubators for new product lines, standards and fundamental infrastructures in an international industry characterized by very short innovation cycles, as well as a fixed component of the innovation strategies of established IT companies.

In the last two decades, OSS projects have thus contributed to more flexibility in the collaboration between developers from divergent contexts, the project-specific cooperation between market actors, as well as inner-organizational production modi—through which the software market as a whole has become more permeable. At the same time, however, freely available source code does not necessarily result in more transparent coordination patterns than in other working contexts, in a disintermediation of the established modes of resource and power distribution over the long term, or a general democratization of innovation processes. In sum, open code alone does not guarantee open societal structures.

Therefore, the prospect that the original concept of commons-based peer production, which was rarely applied as such even in early open source communities, could be adapted to neighboring socio-economic fields such as 3D printing (e.g., Rifkin 2014) and socio-political phenomena such as social movements (e.g., Bennett et al. 2014) remains at best misleading. Worse, these types of narratives deflect from the fact that some trends engendered by the digital transformation of society are not necessarily compatible with the ideal of a more open and democratic economy. We think only of the potential erosion of "the foundations of the system of work and labour regulation as it has developed historically, both on the company and on the society level" (Boes et al. 2017, p. 143), the restriction of fundamental consumer rights through the terms and conditions imposed on the users of many online services, or the global hegemony of a small number of multinational companies over the key infrastructures of communication, media distribution and information retrieval to a degree unprecedented in media history (Schrape 2017, pp. 145–147; Dolata 2017).[7]

Against this background, social scientists would do well to scrutinize popular catchwords such as *Open Innovation*, *Web 2.0* or *Open Source*, often deliberately coined by professional "visioneers" in Silicon Valley or other high-tech hubs (McCray 2013), before adopting them at once as quasi-sociological terms. Instead, efforts should be made to examine to what degree the expectations associated with these terms might point to reoccurring semantic patterns and to assess their societal impacts. For example, even though the "narratives of openness and individual empowerment" (Ames et al. 2014, p. 1088), which are associated with OSS projects and more recent phenomena such as the "maker culture," have not (yet) been brought to fruition as intended, they nevertheless fulfill elementary functions in their respective communicative contexts. Namely, they draw attention to new technological development paths, channel the discourse, contribute to the creation of innovation niches, and serve as a legitimizing basis in economic or political decision-making processes in addition to enhancing the internal cohesiveness of the respective fields. In this respect, the themed openness narratives could indeed qualify as "productive

---

[7]Furthermore, as vendor lock-in is still attractive to vendors, many IT companies are practicing one or another kind of "openwashing" for marketing purposes (Pomerantz and Peek 2016): "Openwashing describes situations where the term 'open' as a (generally positive) adjective actually obscures the fact that content, processes, platforms or institutions are in reality not 'open' or at least not in the ways others think they should be" (Smith and Seward 2017).

types of communication," provided they are not—as was done for a long time by observers of OSS projects—misunderstood as mere descriptions of empirical facts and dynamics (Dickel and Schrape 2017, p. 172).

References

Accelerance Inc. (2017). *Global IT market size: Facts and figures*. http://www.accelerance.com/research/global-it-market-size-facts-and-figures (5/2017). Accessed 21 January 2018.

Ahrne, G., Brunsson, N., & Seidl, D. (2016). Resurrecting organization by going beyond organizations. *European Management Journal, 34*(2), 93–101.

Allen, D. W. E., & Potts, J. (2016). How innovation commons contribute to discovering and developing new technologies. *International Journal of the Commons, 10*(2), 1035–1054.

Allen, R. C. (1983). Collective invention. *Journal of Economic Behavior & Organization, 4*(1), 1–24.

Alphabet Inc. (2016). *Form 10-K 2016*. https://abc.xyz/investor/. Accessed 21 January 2018.

Ames, M., Bardzell, J., Bardzell, S., Lindtner, Mellis, D., & Rosner, D. (2014). Making cultures: Empowerment, participation, and democracy–or not? *Proceedings of the 32nd ACM Conference on Human Factors in Computing Systems* (pp. 1087–1092).

Ante, S. (2014). Red Hat plays hardball on OpenStack software. *The Wall Street Journal*. http://on.wsj.com/14qBpus. Accessed 13 May 2014.

Arrow, K. J. (1962). Economic welfare and the allocation of resources for invention. In R. Nelson (Ed.): *The rate and direction of inventive activity. economic and social factors* (pp. 609–626). Princeton: Princeton University Press.

Benkler, Y. (2002). Coase's Penguin, or, Linux and "The Nature of the Firm". *Yale Law Journal, 112*, 369–446.

Benkler, Y. (2004). Intellectual property: Commons-based strategies and the problems of patents. *Science, 305*(5687), 1110–1111.

Benkler, Y. (2006). *The wealth of networks. How social production transforms markets and freedom*. New Haven: Yale University Press.

Benkler, Y. (2013). Practical anarchism, peer mutualism, market power, and the fallible state. *Politics & Society, 41*(2), 213–251.

Benkler, Y., & Nissenbaum, H. (2006). Commons-based peer production and virtue. *Journal of Political Philosophy, 14*(4), 394–419.

Bennett, W. L., & Segerberg, A. (2015). The logic of connective action: Digital media and the personalization of contentious politics. In S. Coleman & D. Freelon (Eds.), *Handbook of digital politics* (pp. 169–198). Cheltenham: Edward Elgar.

Bennett, W. L., Segerberg, A., & Walker, S. (2014). Organization in the crowd: Peer production in large-scale networked protests. *Information, Communication & Society, 17*(2), 232–260.

Bergquist, M., Ljungberg, J., & Rolandsson, B. (2012). *Justifying the value of open source*. ECIS Proceedings. http://aisel.aisnet.org/ecis2012/122/. Accessed 21 January 2018.

Bezroukov, N. (1999a). A second look at the cathedral and the bazaar. *First Monday*. http://firstmonday.org/article/view/708/618. Accessed 21 January 2018.

Bezroukov N. (1999b). Open source software development as a special type of academic research. *First Monday*. http://journals.uic.edu/ojs/index.php/fm/article/view/696/606. Accessed 21 January 2018.

Blau, P. M., & Scott, R. W. (1962). *Formal organizations. A comparative approach*. San Francisco: Chandler.

Boes, A., Kämpf, T., Langes, B., Lühr, T., & Ziegler, A. (2017). Cloud & crowd: New challenges for labour in the digital society. *tripleC: Communication, Capitalism & Critique, 15(1)*, 132–147.

Brooks, F. (1975). *The mythical man-month*. Reading: Addison-Wesley.

Bulajewski, M. (2011). The peer production illusion, Part I. *MrTeaCup*. http://www.mrteacup.org/post/peer-production-illusion-part-1.html. Accessed 21 January 2018.

Burton, G. (2002). A personal recollection: IBM''s unbundling of software and services. *IEEE Annals of the History of Computing, 24*(3), 64–71.

Byfield, B. (2013). What makes for a community distribution? *Linux Magazine*. http://www.linux-magazine.com/Online/Blogs/Off-the-Beat-Bruce-Byfield-s-Blog/What-makes-for-a-community-distribution. Accessed 13 May 2017.

Cabrera, A., & Cabrera, E. F. (2002). Knowledge-sharing dilemmas. *Organization Studies, 23*(5), 687–710.

Campbell-Kelly, M. (2003). *From airline reservations to Sonic the Hedgehog. A history of the software industry*. Boston: MIT Press.

Coleman, G. (2013). *Coding freedom. The ethics and aesthetics of hacking*. Princeton: Princeton University Press.

Connell, C. (2000). *Open source projects manage themselves? Dream on*. IBM/Lotus Developers Network. http://www.chc-3.com/pub/manage_themselves.htm. Accessed 21 January 2018.

Corbet, J., Kroah-Hartman, G., & McPherson, A. (2009–2015). *Linux kernel development report*. San Francisco: The Linux Foundation.

Corbet, J., & Kroah-Hartman, G. (2016). *Linux kernel development report*. San Francisco: The Linux Foundation.

Corbet, J., & Kroah-Hartman, G. (2017). *Linux kernel development report*. San Francisco: The Linux Foundation.

Dahlander, L., & Magnusson, M. (2008). How do firms make use of open source communities? *Long Range Planning, 41*(6), 629–649.

Dickel, S., & Schrape, J.-F. (2017). The logic of digital utopianism. *Nano Ethics, 11*(1), 47–58.

Dobusch, L., Dobusch, L., Müller-Seiz, G. (2017). Closing for the benefit of openness? The case of Wikimedia's open strategy process. *Organization Studies*, http://journals.sagepub.com/doi/abs/10.1177/0170840617736930.

Dolata, U. (2013). *The transformative capacity of new technologies. A theory of sociotechnical change*. London: Routledge.

Dolata, U. (2017). *Apple, Amazon, Google, Facebook, Microsoft. Market concentration—competition—innovation strategies*. Research Contributions to Organizational Sociology and Innovation Studies 2017–01.

Dolata, U., & Schrape, J.-F. (2016). Masses, crowds, communities, movements: Collective action in the internet age. *Social Movement Studies, 15*(1), 1–18.

Driver, M. (2014). *Within the enterprise, open source must coexist in a hybrid IT portfolio*. Gartner Inc. Research Report. Stamford: Gartner Inc.

Fisher, F. M., McKie, J. W., & Mancke, R. B. (1983). *IBM and the US data processing industry. An economic history*. Santa Barbara: Praeger.

Fitzgerald, B. (2006). The transformation of open source software. *MIS Quarterly, 30*(3), 587–598.

Free Software Foundation. (1989). *GNU General Public License (GPL) Version 1.0*. http://www.gnu.org/licenses/old-licenses/gpl-1.0.en.html. Accessed 21 January 2018.

Gates, B. (1976). An open letter to hobbyists. *Computer Notes, 1*(9), 3.

Geels, F. W., & Schot, J. W. (2007). Typology of sociotechnical transition pathways. *Research Policy, 36*(3), 399–417.

Gelsi, S. (1999, 10 December). VA Linux rockets 698%. *CBS Marketwatch*. http://www.cbsnews.com/news/va-linux-rockets-698/. Accessed 21 January 2018.

GNU Project (2017). *GCC Steering Committee*. https://gcc.gnu.org/steering.html. Accessed 21 January 2018.

Gonzalez-Barahona, J. M., Izquierdo-Cortazar, D., & Maffulli, S. (2013). Understanding how companies interact with free software communities. *IEEE Software, 30*(5), 38–45.

Greenstein, S., & Nagle, F. (2014). Digital dark matter and the economic contribution of Apache. *Research Policy, 43*(4), 623–631.

Gulley, N., & Lakhani, K. (2010). *The determinants of individual performance and collective value in private-collective software innovation*. Harvard BS TOMU Working Paper 10/065.

Hayes, F. (2001). The Microsoft way. *Computerworld*. https://www.computerworld.com/article/2590879/enterprise-applications/the-microsoft-way.html. Accessed 21 January 2018.

Henkel, J., Schöberl, S., & Alexy, O. (2014). The emergence of openness: How and why firms adopt selective revealing in open innovation. *Research Policy, 43*(5), 879–890.

Herstatt, C., & Ehls, D. (2015). *Open source innovation: Phenomenon, participant behaviour, business implications*. New York: Routledge.

Holtgrewe, U., & Werle, R. (2001). De-commodifying software? Open source software between business strategy and social movement. *Science Studies, 14*(2), 43–65.

Jaeger, T. (2010). Enforcement of the GNU GPL in Germany and Europe. *Journal of Intellectual Property, Information Technology and E-Commerce Law, 1*(1), 34–39.

Jewkes, J., Sawyers, D., & Stillerman, R. (1969). *The sources of invention* (Vol. 2). London: Palgrave Macmillan.

KDE Project. (2017). *Project management*. https://www.kde.org/community/whatiskde/management.php. Accessed 21 January 2018.

Kernel.Org. (2016). *How to get your change into the Linux kernel*. https://www.kernel.org/doc/Documentation/process/submitting-patches.rst. Accessed 21 January 2018.

Kolassa, C., Riehle, D., Riemer, P., & Schmidt, M. (2014). Paid vs. volunteer work in open source. In *Proceedings 47th Hawaii Int. Conference on System Sciences* (pp. 3286–3295).

Kostakis, V., Niaros, V., & Giotitsas, C. (2015). Production and governance in hackerspaces: A manifestation of commons-based peer production in the physical realm? *International Journal of Cultural Studies, 18*(5), 555–573.

Kreiss, D., Finn, M., & Turner, F. (2011). The limits of peer production: Some reminders from Max Weber for the network society. *New Media & Society, 13*(2), 243–259.

Lakhani, K. R., & von Hippel, E. (2003). How open source software works. *Research Policy, 32*(6), 923–943.

Lamoreaux, N. R., & Sokoloff, K. L. (2000). The geography of invention in the American glass industry 1870–1925. *Journal of Economic History, 60*(3), 700–729.

Larsson, R., Bengtsson, L., Henriksson, K., & Sparks, J. (1998). The interorganizational learning dilemma: Collective knowledge development in strategic alliances. *Organization Science, 9*(3), 285–305.

Lerner, J. (2012). *The architecture of innovation*. Boston: Harvard Business Press.

Lerner, J., & Schankerman, M. (2010). *The comingled code. Open source and economic development*. Cambridge: MIT Press.

Lerner, J., & Tirole, J. (2002). Some simple economics of open source. *Journal of Industrial Economics, 50*(2), 197–234.

Lerner, J., & Tirole, J. (2005). The scope of open source licensing. *Journal of Law Economics and Organization, 21*(1), 20–56.

Lessig, L. (1999). Open code and open societies. *Chicago Kent Law Review, 74*, 1405–1420.

Levy, S. (1984). *Hackers. Heroes of the computer revolution*. Garden City: Anchor Press.

Levine, P. (2014). Why there will never be another Red Hat: The economics of open source. *Techcrunch*. http://tcrn.ch/1bs5yMQ. Accessed 21 January 2018.

Lowood, H. (2009). Videogames in computer space: The complex history of Pong. *IEEE Annals of the History of Computing, 31*(3), 5–19.

Martin, J. (1991). *Rapid application development*. Indianapolis: Macmillan.

Mason, P. (2015). *PostCapitalism: A guide to our future*. London: Allen Lane.

Mayntz, R. (2004). Mechanisms in the analysis of social macro-phenomena. *Philosophy of the Social Sciences, 34*(2), 237–259.

McCray, P. W. (2013). *The visioneers. How a group of elite scientists pursued space colonies, nanotechnologies, and a limitless future*. Princeton: Princeton University Press.

McGaw, J. A. (1987). *Most wonderful machine: Mechanization and social change in Berkshire paper making 1801–1885*. Princeton: Princeton University Press.

Menell, P. S. (2002). Envisioning copyright law's digital future. *New York Law School Review, 46,* 63–199.

Meyer, P. B. (2003). *Episodes of collective invention.* BLS Working Paper 368. Washington: U.S. Bureau of Labor Statistics.

Microsoft Inc. (2017). *2016 Annual Report.* http://www.microsoft.com/investor/reports/. 21 January 2018.

Miller, P., & Nelson, L. E. (2016). *Open source powers enterprise digital transformation.* Cambridge: Forrester Inc. (Research Report).

Moody, G. (2002). *Rebel code. The inside story of Linux and the open source revolution.* New York: Basic Books.

Mozilla Foundation. (2016). *Mozilla Wiki WeeklyUpdates.* https://wiki.mozilla.org/WeeklyUpdates. Accessed 21 January 2018.

Netscape Communications. (1998). *Netscape announces Mozilla.org.* Press Release from 23 February 1998.

Nuvolari, A. (2004). Collective invention during the British industrial revolution: The case of the Cornish pumping engine. *Cambridge Journal of Economics, 28*(3), 347–363.

O'Mahony, S. (2003). Guarding the commons. How community managed software projects protect their work. *Research Policy, 32*(7), 1179–1198.

O'Mahony, S., & Ferraro, F. (2007). The emergence of governance in an open source community. *Academy of Management Journal, 50*(5), 1079–1106.

O'Reilly, T. (2000). *Re: Open Source and OpenGL.* Ask Tim Forum. http://archive.oreilly.com/pub/a/oreilly/ask_tim/2000/opengl_1200.html. 21 January 2018.

Osterloh, M., & Rota, S. (2007). Open source software development: Just another case of collective invention? *Research Policy, 36*(2), 157–171.

Perlroth, N. (2014, April 18). Heartbleed highlights a contradiction in the web. *The New York Times.* http://nyti.ms/1hb6uBd. Accessed 21 January 2018.

Perrow, C. (1991). A society of organizations. *Theory & Society, 20,* 725–762.

Pomerantz, J., & Peek, R. (2016). Fifty shades of open. *First Monday.* http://dx.doi.org/10.5210/fm.v21i5.6360. Accessed 21 January 2018.

Powell, W. W., & Giannella, E. (2010). Collective invention and inventor networks. In B. H. Hall & N. Rosenberg (Eds.), *Handbook of the economics of innovation* (Vol. 1, pp. 575–605). Oxford: Elsevier.

Raymond, E. S. (1998, 22 November). Goodbye, "free software"; Hello, "open source". *Eric's Home Page.* ftp://ftp.lab.unb.br/pub/computing/museum/esr/open-source.html. Accessed 21 January 2018.

Raymond, E. S. (1999). *The cathedral and the bazaar. Musings on Linux and open source by an accidental revolutionary.* Sebastopol: O'Reilly.

Rifkin, J. (2014). *The zero marginal cost society.* New York: Palgrave Macmillan.

Romer, P. (1990). Endogenous technological change. *Journal of Political Economy, 98*(5), 71–102.

Schrape, J.-F. (2017). Reciprocal irritations: Social media, mass media and the public sphere. In R. Paul, M. Mölders, A. Bora, M. Huber, & P. Münte (Eds.), *Society, regulation and governance: New modes of shaping social change?* (pp. 138–149). Cheltenham: Edward Elgar Publishing.

Scott, W. R. (2004). Reflections on a half-century of organizational sociology. *Annual Review of Sociology, 30*(1), 1–21.

Scranton, P. (1997). *Endless novelty: Specialty production and American industrialization 1865–1925.* Princeton: Princeton University Press.

Smith, L., & Seward, R. (2017). Openness as social praxis. *First Monday.* https://firstmonday.org/ojs/index.php/fm/article/view/7073/6087. Accessed 21 January 2018.

Snow, S. (2014). How Matt's machine works. *Fast Company.* http://www.fastcompany.com/3035463/how-matts-machine-works. Accessed 21 January 2018.

Spencer, J. W. (2003). Firms' knowledge-sharing strategies in the global innovation system. Evidence from the flat panel display industry. *Strategic Management Journal, 24*(3), 217–233.

Spinellis, D., & Giannikas, V. (2012). Organizational adoption of open source software. *Journal of Systems and Software, 85*(3), 666–682.

Spreeuwenberg, K., & Poell, T. (2012). Android and the political economy of the mobile internet. *First Monday*. https://doi.org/10.5210/fm.v17i7.4050.

Stallman, R. (1983). *New UNIX implementation*. http://bit.ly/1DSDoXW. Accessed 21 January 2018.

Stallman, R. (2002). *Free software, free society*. Boston: GNU Press.

Stamelos, I. (2014). Management and coordination of free/open source projects. In G. Ruhe & C. Wohlin (Eds.), *Software project management in a changing world* (pp. 321–341). New York: Springer.

Steinberg J. (2014). Massive internet security vulnerability. *Forbes*. https://www.forbes.com/sites/josephsteinberg/2014/04/10/massive-internet-security-vulnerability-you-are-at-risk-what-you-need-to-do/. Accessed 21 January 2018.

Steinmacher, I., Conte, T., Redmiles, D., & Gerosa, M. (2015). Social barriers faced by newcomers placing their first contribution in open source software projects. *Proceedings of the 18th ACM Conference on Computer Supported Cooperative Work & Social Computing* (pp. 1379–1392).

Stiller, A. (2011). The open source trials: Hanging in the legal balance of copyright and copyleft. *Vision Mobile Blog*. http://www.visionmobile.com/blog/2011/03/the-open-source-trials-hanging-in-the-legal-balance-of-copyright-and-copyleft/. Accessed 21 January 2018.

Stokel-Walker, C. (2014). The internet is being protected by two guys named Steve. *Buzzfeed*. https://www.buzzfeed.com/chrisstokelwalker/the-internet-is-being-protected-by-two-guys-named-st?utm_term=.nqdX2Jd0K#.rfBqKaY5V. Accessed 21 January 2018.

Suddaby, R. (2013). Book review: The Janus face of commercial open source software communities. *Organization Studies, 34*(7), 1009–1011.

Sydow, J., Schüssler, E., & Müller-Seitz, G. (2016). *Managing inter-organizational relations: Debates and cases*. London: Palgrave Macmillan.

Tapscott, D., & Williams, A. D. (2006). *Wikinomics. How mass collaboration changes everything*. New York: Portfolio.

Torvalds, L. (1998). *LINUX manifesto. Interview. Boot Magazine, 1998*(7–8), 32–37.

Torvalds, L. (2002). *Re: [PATCH] remove bitkeeper documentation from Linux tree*. Linux Kernel Mailinglist 20 April 2002. http://lwn.net/2002/0425/a/ideology-sucks.php3. Accessed 21 January 2018.

Ubuntu Project. (2017). *Governance*. https://www.ubuntu.com/about/about-ubuntu/governance. Accessed 21 January 2018.

UNCTAD—United Nations Conference of Trade and Development. (2012). *Information economy report 2012*. New York/Geneva: United Nations.

van de Ven, A. H., Delbecq, A. L., & Koenig, R., Jr. (1976). Determinants of coordination modes within organizations. *American Sociological Review, 41*(2), 322–338.

Weber, S. (2000). *The political economy of open source*. BRIE Working Paper 140. Berkeley: University of California.

Weinberg, B. (2015a). The internet of things and open source. In I. Podnar Žarko, K. Pripužić, M. Serrano (Eds.), *Interoperability and open-source solutions for the internet of things* (pp. 1–5). Lecture notes in computer science No. 9001. Cham: Springer.

Weinberg, B. (2015b). *Open source and the internet of things: A reality check*. http://blog.blackducksoftware.com/open-source-and-the-internet-of-things-a-reality-check. Accessed 21 January 2018.

West, J., & Bogers, M. (2014). Leveraging external sources of innovation. A review of research on open innovation. *Journal of Product Innovation Management, 31*(4), 814–831.

West, J., & Bogers, M. (2017). Open innovation: Current status and research opportunities. *Innovation, 19*(1), 43–50.

Chapter 5
Internet Companies: Market Concentration, Competition and Power

Ulrich Dolata

Abstract Based on a systematic review and evaluation of business reports, documents, statistics, literature and press releases, this article analyzes the market concentration and the expansion and innovation strategies of the leading internet companies Google, Facebook, Apple, Amazon and Microsoft. The findings invalidate any claims that a decentralization of the market and a democratization of the internet is taking place, or that research, development and innovation processes are becoming more open and collaborative. The five examined companies, as the operators of the core infrastructures of the worldwide web, shape the overall products and services offer of the internet, determine access to the web, structure the communication possibilities for users, and are the main drivers of innovation in this field. Not decentralization, democratization and open innovation but market concentration, control and power struggles are categories to adequately describe the fundamental dynamics of the commercial internet.

Keywords Internet economy · Digital capitalism · Platforms
Innovation · Market concentration · Power · Regulation

1 Introduction

Over the past two decades, the internet has evolved into a ubiquitous information, communication and media network that is indispensable to the social reality of our societies. Its visible interface includes search engines, e-commerce platforms and social media services as distinct commercial offers. It is on these platforms that the bulk of information provision, consumption, user-generated content and private or public exchange on the internet takes place. In addition there are multi-function and mobile devices such as smartphones, tablets or laptops which serve as means of access or communication. The vastly invisible but nonetheless structuring footing of this extensive infrastructure is formed by a diverse range of software applications with which operators not only manage, aggregate and evaluate large amounts of data but also direct the actions, and modes of action, of the individual platforms.

© The Author(s) 2018
U. Dolata and J.-F. Schrape, *Collectivity and Power on the Internet*,
SpringerBriefs in Sociology, https://doi.org/10.1007/978-3-319-78414-4_5

Although the internet still provides room for decentralized and collaborative production and innovation processes, or the emergence of start-ups such as Spotify, Airbnb or Uber, large parts of the web are now dominated by the offerings of a few leading internet companies, all of which are based in the United States. These are, by and large, Google (restructured into "Alphabet" in 2015), Facebook, Amazon, Apple and Microsoft. They not only dominate the basic offerings and markets of the internet, but, as operators of the central infrastructures, also regulate access to the web, structure the communication possibilities of users, are key drivers of the innovation process and, as employers of some 10,000 or 100,000 staff, shape the working conditions of the commercial internet sector. With the exception of Facebook, these companies are among the 50 companies with the highest revenues in the United States. Indeed, in 2016, Apple ranked 3rd, Amazon 12th, Google 27th, Microsoft 28th and Facebook 98th in terms of revenues (Table 1, Fortune 500, 2017).

The focus of this article, which is based on the analysis of business reports, documents, empirical material, literature and press reports, is on the economic, infrastructural and rule-setting power that these companies have acquired by now. The findings presented repudiate the existence of the supposed decentralization of the market and the democratization of innovation processes just as much as the notions of a largely open and collaborative technology and product development (Chesbrough 2003a, b; von Hippel 2005; Benkler 2006; Tapscott and Williams 2006). Not decentralization, democratization and cooperation but rather concentration, control and power are—which comprises the thesis of this article—the key processes and categories with which to adequately describe the essential development trends of the (commercial) internet.

This article is structured as follows. First, we examine the concentration processes in important segments and markets of the internet (Sect. 2), followed by an analysis of the main modes of expansion and competition between the big internet companies (Sect. 3). An overall dense concentration of the supply and the market is accompanied by fierce oligopolistic competition between the leading companies. This competition is fought out primarily by way of innovative leads. Given the important role of innovation, Sect. 4 analyzes and systematizes these groups' innovation strategies. The latter are still characterized by a strong in-house orientation, for two main reasons. For one, strategically relevant projects are carried out at the companies' own research and development (R&D) centers under tightly controlled conditions of strict secrecy and, secondly, external know-how is obtained primarily through acquisitions and then integrated into the companies' own research. Section 5 summarizes the expansion and innovation strategies of the big internet companies and discusses the question of how their dominance is reflected not only in economic clout but also in data-related, infrastructural and rule-setting power.

Table 1 Internet companies—economic data 2017

Company	Revenue 2017	Net Income 2017	Core business	R&D 2017	Share R&D in revenue	Employees 2017
fiscal year end	in billion US$	in billion US$	in billion US$	in billion US$	in %	in thousands
Apple (9/2017)	229.2	48.4	186.4 Hardware[a] (81%)	11.6	5.1	123,000
Amazon (12/2017)	177.9	3.0	147.7 Retail[b] (83%)	22.6[c]	12.7	566,000
Google[d] (12/2017)	110.9	12.7	95.4 Advertising (86%)	16.6	15.0	80,110
Microsoft (6/2017)	90.0	21.2	73.2 Software/Services[e] (81%)	13.0	14.4	124,000
Facebook (12/2017)	40.7	15.9	40.0 Advertising (98%)	7.8	19.2	25,105

[a]iPhone, iPad and Mac
[b]Total revenue less sales with AWS, subscription services and other
[c]Amazon conducts its R&D under the "Technology and Content" label, which is much more than just research and development: "Technology costs consist principally of research and development activities, including payroll and related expenses for employees involved in application, production, maintenance, operation and platform development for new and existing products and services, as well as AWS and other technology infrastructure expenses. Content costs consist principally of payroll and related expenses for employees involved in category expansion, editorial content, buying and merchandising selection" (Amazon.com Inc 2013, pp. 27, 42)
[d]Alphabet Inc. since 2015
[e]Rough estimation: Total revenue less sales with devices (computing, gaming and phone hardware)
Source 2017/18 Annual Reports (Form 10-K) of the companies; own compilation

2 Concentration: Market Power and the Fight to Secure Business Sectors

Economically speaking, the internet is not a clearly defined sector with a well-developed data basis (such as the automotive or pharmaceutical industry). Instead it offers the space for relatively few yet commercially diverse activities, especially in advertising, commerce, mediation services and the sale of multi-function devices. The market structures on the internet likewise differ from those of many classic markets. Often the companies here act as intermediaries in so-called two-sided markets in which the commercial attractiveness of offerings, for example to advertisers or retailers, on one side of the market depends directly on the number of regularly active users of their free services on the other side of the market. This effect is particularly noticeable in search engines or social networking platforms. Indeed, the economic success of Google and Facebook as advertising and marketing companies results from the large number of users, which make these platforms particularly interesting for advertisers. Commercial or mediation platforms such as Amazon, booking.com or Airbnb likewise work according to this principle (Rochet and Tirole 2003).

A look at the most important segments and markets of the commercial internet shows that each of the companies examined in this study has carved out its own domain.[1]

The *search engine* segment is globally dominated by Google as a quasi-monopolist. In all leading Western countries, Google is the unchallenged monopolist in this field—usually accounting for well more than 90% of all search queries (Netmarketshare 2017a). Even the once promising search engines Yahoo or Bing, of Microsoft, are today insignificant. Moreover, numerous smaller and specialized search engine providers are now generating their results via Google.

In the *social networks* sector, Facebook had evolved from a newcomer to a world-wide dominant company in only a few years, ousting former platforms such as MySpace or, in Germany, StudiVZ along the way. At the End of 2017, some 2.1 billion people were registered as monthly active users on Facebook, about 1.5 billion on WhatsApp and 800 million on Instagram (Facebook 2018). Facebook, and its two subsidiaries, presently dominate the social networks sector just as much as Google does the search engine market.

Search engines and social networks are not markets; however, they form the basis of the core business of Google and Facebook. In fact, the two companies generate the bulk of their revenue through *internet advertising* (Table 1), which is a fast-growing and highly concentrated market (Evans 2008). In the United States, this market accounted for one third (33%) of all advertising revenues, or $59.6 billion, in 2015 (and $72.5 billion in 2016). Only television advertising (Broadcast and Cable Television) generated more revenues in 2015, namely $66.3 billion. At the End of 2016 in the United States, 73% of the total revenue generated by advertising on the internet was realized by the top ten advertising companies in this sector. And Google, which makes 47% of its revenue in the United States, captured approximately 50% of that total revenue. Worldwide, too, this segment is clearly dominated by Google, followed by Facebook (PriceWaterhouseCoopers 2016, 2017; Table 1). Nonetheless, Google would not qualify as a monopolist in this market, being challenged in particular by Facebook. It should be stated, moreover, that internet advertising is still competing with other advertising media such as television, radio and magazines.

E-commerce is the domain of Amazon, by far the largest retailer on the internet (Stone 2013; National Retail Federation 2017a). In the United States, Amazon in

---

[1]The use of the term *commercial internet* refers to consumer-oriented economic offerings and markets, which is referred to as business-to-consumer (B2C) e-commerce in the economic literature. The internet companies examined here are predominantly active in this B2C sector. The latter is in fact relatively small compared to e-commerce as a whole, as that includes the economic activities taking place between companies (business-to-business e-commerce, B2B). "While the internet economy is generally thought of as enterprises selling to consumers, the vast majority of e-commerce is actually comprised of businesses selling to other businesses. In 2007, roughly 90% of global e-commerce was B2B" (Atkinson et al. 2010, p. 22).

2017 accounted for an estimated 43% of total e-commerce sales, followed by eBay (6.8%), Wal-Mart (3.6%) and Apple (3.6%) (Garcia 2017). Here too, the effects of two-sided markets are evident: the more consumers use Amazon, the more interesting the platform becomes for retailers—and the more Amazon can dictate the conditions under which these can make their offerings there. It should be noted, however, that e-commerce retail, with a turnover of around 9% of all retail trade, is still a small segment of retail at large, which is still dominated by classic brick-and-mortar retail companies (like Walmart). Nonetheless, in 2017 Amazon ranked 7th among the largest retailers in the United States (National Retail Federation 2017b).

Apple, for its part, has burgeoned since the early 2000s from a niche provider for PCs to the leading and trend-defining manufacturer in the *multimedia devices market*: iPod and iTunes were constitutive of the internet-based music market; the iPhone and the proprietary operating system iOS led to the triumph of smartphones; and with the iPad Apple pioneered the market for tablet PCs. This was accompanied with a sky-rocketing increase in revenue from $5.4 billion (2001) to $229 billion (2017). Nevertheless, even in its rather classically-oriented consumer markets Apple is not a monopolist and is under immense pressure from its competitors. The extremely dynamic and fiercely competitive mobile devices market, previously in the hands of Nokia, has been dominated since the advent of smartphones by Apple and the South Korean company Samsung Electronics. That said, looking at the number of smartphones sold worldwide in 2017, Apple and Samsung together accounted for just under 40% of all sales, followed by a number of smaller competitors such as Huawei (IDC 2017). By contrast, in the field of *mobile device operating systems*, Google and Apple have been the central players, and competitors, for several years. In 2017, 69% of all devices were equipped with Google's open Android system and 29% with Apple's proprietary iOS system (Netmarketshare 2017b).

Although the commercial internet is a relatively new phenomenon, its cornerstones (consumer-oriented commerce, advertising, services, equipment and software) are now dominated by a few companies—not just nationally but internationally. This is due to various factors which, in their interaction, explain the high degree of concentration in the different business sectors of the internet.

For many internet offerings, direct or indirect *network effects* are typical. The allegedly egalitarian and decentralized web produces, even under normal circumstances, only few centralized sites for doing searches and engaging in communication, networking and consumption, attributed to the similar behavior of the numerous users (Barabasi and Bonabeau 2003). These sites essentially comprise social media platforms such as Facebook, YouTube and Twitter. The more such web services are used and the more members they have, the more interesting they become for additional users who then flock there—and the more difficult it becomes for alternative providers to compete. E-commerce platforms or search engines can likewise benefit from such network effects. For example, an e-commerce platform like Amazon can easily attract additional users due to its high acceptance and broad product range. For those same reasons, a leading search engine such as Google can generate added trust in the superior quality of its search results and thereby attract new users. In addition, given the mass of data which Google generates over the long term, the company can continually improve the quality of the search algorithm, thereby distinguishing itself from the competition. Such network effects result in quasi-monopolies, which are engendered by the mass behavior on the web in addition to being, often, desired by the users (Shelanski 2013; Monopolkommission 2014).

However, not only massively streamlined behavior of users can produce such Matthew effects. The reach and reputation of an offer also entails indirect network effects, which are triggered by actors on the other side of the market (Haucap and Wenzel 2011; Haucap and Heimeshoff 2014). A dominant social network or a frequently used search engine, for example, is of particular interest to advertisers, as it allows them to bundle their advertising activities, which in turn contributes to the concentration of the advertising market on the internet. A leading retailer such as Amazon also becomes a coveted intermediary and e-commerce platform for other retailers who wish to benefit from the high visibility of this established online retailer. Finally, the heavily frequented app stores such as those of Google and Apple are instrumental in shaping the ways in which end users select and purchase their devices, while also becoming the preferred venue for numerous software developers wishing to present and market their applications there.

Network effects of this kind can be augmented if the switch from one offer to another is associated with comparatively high *switching costs* (Pollock 2010). All companies work hard to keep users, customers, providers and advertisers tied as extensively and permanently as possible to their services. As a result, proprietary system environments, such as those provided by Apple and Amazon with their customized and integrated hardware offerings, programs and services, are designed to prevent any subsequent systems change and to aim for exclusive use. Even open systems such as Google's operating system Android for mobile devices can produce such lock-in effects. The purchase of a smartphone or tablet is linked to the choice between two operating systems (and app stores), which are not only mutually incompatible but which also differ greatly with regard to their interface concepts and usage routines.

However, what contributes the most to the increase of switching costs for users and providers is the development of the various offerings and business activities into integrated sociotechnical ecosystems that encompass coordinated and networked services, programs and devices. Such ecosystems are not simply cross-application technological infrastructures but rather, with their wide range of offerings and services, also social spaces in which users build member profiles, establish specific search, communication and consumption patterns, and develop reproducible usage routines—all of which invariably ties them to the offerings of a given company. Overall, users do have the possibility to switch systems, yet only at the price of a comprehensive reorganization or reconstitution of their individual patterns and movements on the web.

In the context of their ecosystems, the internet companies also act as *active market creators and regulators*. Amazon's e-commerce platform, for example, has long since integrated a number of independent retailers. Similarly, Google's video platform YouTube is now much more than the playground for amateurs it started out as. Rather, it is an advertising market place used by big-name companies as well as by

Table 2 Stock market value of selected internet companies (January 12, 2018)

	Stock market value *in billion US$*
Apple	900.9
Google	785.6
Microsoft	691.2
Amazon	629.0
Facebook	521.2

Source NASDAQ: Market Cap on January 12, 2018

numerous professional YouTubers, many with their own firms. Finally, the app stores operated by the big companies have become the focus of activity for many more or less successful developers. As a result, the scope and reach of the internet companies has grown beyond their activities in existing markets. As platform operators, they also create, organize, regulate and control markets and market competition within their ecosystems (Kenney and Zysman 2016; Srnicek 2017; Kirchner and Beyer 2016).

In addition, another factor plays a central role in the concentration dynamics and the consolidation of market power on the internet: the *superior economic resources* which the leading internet companies can now put into play to stabilize and expand their market power. These consist of high stock market values and considerable liquid assets that enable these companies to make major investments and costly acquisitions on a continual basis (Table 2).

Due to their extraordinary financial strength, the internet companies are in a position to invest heavily in the continuous development of their own *technological and logistical infrastructures*. The latter may include: server architectures; data collection and evaluation technologies; the quality of search algorithms; the technical integration of extensive ecosystems; or, as in the case of Amazon, the group's ordering, logistics and warehouse systems. This alone makes it very hard for newcomers to become serious competitors of the established leaders in any of the already occupied core business fields.

In addition, all internet groups have the necessary financial resources to continually and consistently invest in their own *research and development* (R&D). This applies not only to the continuous and frequent improvement of their already established product and service portfolio but also to technology and innovation fields that are new to those companies and with which they hope to gradually expand their radius of action. In highly dynamic and fast-moving technology markets such as those discussed here, where competitive positions are often defined less by price than by innovation strategies and innovation leadership, this ability to make massive investments in R&D becomes a key competitive advantage against newcomers.

Last but not least, any of these companies are easily able to protect their business fields and to penetrate into new sectors not only through internal restructuring but also through at times very costly *partnerships and acquisitions* (Hong et al. 2013; Table 3). The vast majority of the numerous smaller "business-as-usual" acquisitions made by all of these companies on a regular basis serve to acquire know-how and interesting applications that support the respective core business. In addition, the acquisition strategies are designed to allow these companies to expand and venture into new business areas. This is typical for the newer company acquisitions of Google (e.g., Nestlabs, Skybox Imaging, Deep Mind), Amazon (e.g., Lovefilm, Double Helix Games, Twitch, Whole Foods), Facebook (e.g., Oculus) and Microsoft (e.g., aQuantive, Skype Technologies, Nokia Devices, LinkedIn). After all, the acquisition of particularly successful newcomers is a tried and tested means to take potential competitors out of the race at an early stage and to integrate their services into one's own group. This is perhaps best illustrated with the purchase of WhatsApp by Facebook in early 2014 (Dolata and Schrape 2014).

3   Expansion: Competition and New Areas of Rivalry

However, the brief history of the commercial internet is characterized not only by a strong trend of mergers and the formation of a few dominant companies. What strikes just as much is the persistently fierce competition over innovation and, in some cases, the swift replacement of market leaders who once seemed indomitable by new players.

As a matter of example, in the early 2000s, the search engine pioneers Altavista, Lycos and Yahoo were quickly crowded out by Google, followed by, a decade later, the ousting of the initial social network pioneers MySpace and StudiVZ (a German student-based social networking platform) by the then-newcomer Facebook—despite the fact that MySpace was owned by News Corporation and StudiVZ by the Holtzbrinck Publishing Group, both powerful media groups. Since the beginning of the 2010s, Facebook has emerged, practically starting from nowhere, as a serious new competitor for Google in the internet advertising market. And in the market for accommodation and car transportation services, Airbnb and Uber have recently positioned themselves as new providers and competitors.

In these cases, newcomers who had until then been unknown became challengers, if not leaders, in those markets. By contrast, the struggle for dominance in the mobile internet market took place between already established groups. For example, the leading providers Nokia and BlackBerry were put in their place, in the late 2000s, by Samsung and Apple; and the competition over mobile operating systems and apps was limited to Apple and Google (Arthur 2012; Angwin 2009; Kirkpatrick 2010).

This means that the strong, sometimes monopolistic position enjoyed by a small number of internet companies is no guarantee for sustained periods of market dominance. This is partly due to the often volatile and unpredictable *behavior of large user groups*. The consumer-oriented product markets and service offerings that characterize the commercial internet are, to a large extent, dependent on the respective preferences of end consumers and users, similar to comparable markets in the old economy.

Table 3 Internet companies—selected mergers and acquisitions

	Year	Company	Purchase price In billion US$
Google	2004	Picasa (photo service)	0.01
	2004	Where 2 Technology (mapping service)	n/a
	2005	Android (mobile software)	0.05
	2006	YouTube (videos, media)	1.65
	2008	Doubleclick (internet advertising)	3.10
	2009	Admob (mobile advertising)	0.75
	2011	Motorola Mobility (mobile devices; 2014 sale to Lenovo for US$ 2.9 billion)	12.50
	2013	Waze (GPS navigation software)	0.97
	2013	Boston Dynamics (military robots)	n/a
	2014	Nest Labs (thermostats; fire alarms)	3.20
	2014	Skybox Imaging (satellite technology)	0.50
	2014	Deep Mind Techn. (artificial intelligence)	0.80
	2016	Apigee (predictive analytics)	0.63
Facebook	2009	FriendFeed (social networking aggregator)	0.05
	2010	Hot Potato (social media platform)	0.01
	2011	Beluga (messaging)	0.01
	2011	Gowalla (social network)	n/a
	2011	Snaptu (app developer)	0.07
	2012	Instagram (photo and video portal)	1.00
	2013	Parse (app platform)	0.09
	2014	WhatsApp (messaging service)	19.00
	2014	Oculus VR (virtual reality)	2.00
	2015	Surreal Vision (augmented reality)	n/a
	2015	Pebbles (augmented reality)	0.06
Amazon	1999	Junglee (online shop; electronics, clothing, books)	0.19
	1999	Alexa Internet (server; website rankings)	0.25
	2008	Audible (audio book download provider)	0.22
	2009	Zappos.com (online shop; shoes, clothing)	0.82

(continued)

Table 3 (continued)

	2010	Quisidi (online shop; drug store, pet food)	0.55
	2011	Living Social (special offers; gift cards)	0.40
	2011	Lovefilm (video rental)	0.30
	2012	Kiva Systems (automatic ordering systems)	0.78
	2013	Goodreads (book community)	0.20
	2014	Double Helix Games (video games)	n/a
	2014	Twitch (video game platform)	0.97
	2016	Curse (game portal)	n/a
	2017	Whole Foods Market (food retailing)	13.70
Apple	1996	Next Computer (software; operating systems)	0.40
	1997	Power Computing (computer manufacturer)	0.11
	2010	Siri (voice assistant software)	0.20
	2012	AuthenTec (biometrics hardware)	0.36
	2013	Topsy Labs (media research)	0.20
	2013	PrimeSense (3D sensor manufacturer)	0.35
	2014	Beats Electronics (headsets; music streaming)	3.00
	2016	Turi (machine learning)	0.20
	2017	Shazam (music and image recognition)	0.40
Microsoft	1997	Hotmail (internet software)	0.50
	2000	Visio Corp. (software)	1.38
	2002	Navision (software)	1.33
	2007	aQuantive (advertising)	6.33
	2008	Fast Search & Transfer (search software for companies)	1.19
	2011	Skype Technologies (voice over IP)	8.50
	2013	Nokia Devices (mobile devices)	7.20
	2014	Mojang (video games)	2.50
	2016	LinkedIn (social network)	26.20

Source Annual reports of the companies; media content analysis; own compilation

This applies to the purchase of technological devices (such as smartphones or tablets) as well as to the use of specific internet services such as search engines, social networks, messaging services and apps. The success of Google's search engine; the dominance of Facebook as a social media network; the rapid increase in the significance of the messaging service WhatsApp, acquired by Facebook; the increased practice of streaming digital music; and the success of vendor-specific smartphones, e-book readers or tablets—what these have in common is that they are all based on user and consumption choices that, by and large, condense in a non-organized and spontaneous manner into mass behavior, and which the companies are then tasked to anticipate and channel (Dolata and Schrape 2016). Indeed, the fact that the swarm can move on is the downside of the described network effects.

To compound matters, given the extraordinary innovation dynamics and rapid trend changes on the commercial internet, the leading companies are constantly challenged to defend and renew their position of dominance. They do so mainly through the development of new offerings and features as well as rapid advances into new growth markets. This means that the companies must demonstrate a high and sustained level of *adaptability*, considered to be comprised of the early and continuous anticipation, reception and integration of new technological and socio-economic developments as well as their implementation into attractive commercial offers (Dolata 2013). The literature on organizational inertia and path dependency has demonstrated that established and saturated companies often underestimate the potential reach or shattering effect of radically new developments, that they are reluctant to veer from the strategic behavior that led to their initial success, and that they are not inclined to adopt new and ambiguous developments unless these are clearly being backed at a broader scale (Mellahi and Wilkinson 2004).

These characteristics by no means apply to all the already established companies. While Apple, Google or Amazon proved to be very adaptable in the last decade, other companies did not. Yahoo's decline from search engine pioneer to takeover target, Nokia's rapid loss of clout in the mobile device market, and Microsoft's ongoing problems with the internet as a whole are examples of how well-established companies do not necessarily succeed in anticipating new trends and in responding promptly with appropriate strategic repositionings (Arthur 2012; Shapiro and Varian 1999).

In addition, the *ambition of internet companies to expand* beyond their regular area of business often leads to new and fierce competition both among themselves and with established media, consumer electronics, technology and industrial enterprises. All the companies considered in this study have been, to a greater or lesser degree, expanding their radius of action for several years. Overall, four key expansion trends and new fields of competition can be identified that are being pushed forward by the companies by means of internal development strategies as well as acquisitions and strategic alliances (Table 4).

The first of these expansion trends concerns the extremely complex field of *internet-based media content and services*, targeted and vied for especially by Google, Apple and Amazon, recently also by Facebook (Dolata and Schrape 2013). Over the last decade, these companies have gradually turned into internet-based media groups and are steadily building their profile as turnkey providers of a broad range of commercial services and media content, some of which they are now producing themselves. Apple had already entered this segment in 2003 by introducing its iTunes music store, and Google in 2006 with the acquisition of the video platform YouTube. Amazon, for its part, has been pursuing the trend since the late 2000s with a very aggressive expansion strategy. In the meantime, Google, Apple and Amazon have a broad portfolio of media offerings consisting of their own digital music and video services (purchase, rental and streaming), e-book and games, app stores as well as over-the-internet access to television. Through these offers they are encroaching

Table 4   Internet companies—areas of expansion and main competitors

	Domain	Expansion	Main competitors
Google	Search engine/ advertising	*Media* YouTube (video/film), Google Play (media-/app store), All Access (music), Google Books *Mobile soft- and hardware* Android, Chrome Browser, Chromecast, Nexus (smartphone and tablet), set-top box running Google TV *Social networks* Google+ *Internet of Things* Smart home, connected car, special drones, artificial intelligence	*Advertising* Facebook, advertising firms *Media* Apple, Amazon, Netflix, Hulu, media companies *Social Networks* Facebook, Twitter, Flickr *Mobile soft- and hardware* Apple, Amazon, Microsoft *Connected car* Apple, car manufacturers *Smart home* Microsoft, Cisco, appliance manufacturers
Facebook	Social network/ advertising	*Media* Instagram (photos), WhatsApp (messaging) *Software* Oculus, Pebbles (virtual reality headsets; augmented reality)	*Advertising* Google, advertising firms *Social networks* Google+, YouTube, Twitter, Flickr, Snapchat *Apps* Google, Apple
Amazon	Retail	*Media* Amazon Game Studios, Lovefilm, Prime Instant Video, Fire TV, Amazon MP3, Amazon Publishing, Amazon App Store *Mobile soft- and hardware* Kindle e-book reader; Kindle Fire tablet, Amazon Fire set-top box (TV) and Fire TV-stick Cloud/IT Leasing Amazon Web Services (AWS)	*Trade* Retail companies, specialized online dealers *Media* Google, Apple, Microsoft, Netflix, Spotify, game manufacturers, media companies *Mobile hardware* Apple, mobile device manufacturers IT Services Microsoft, IBM, Apple, Google
Apple	Consumer/communications-electronics	*Media* iTunes Store, App Store, iBooks Store, Apple TV set-top box, music-streaming *Mobile hard- and software* iPhone, iPad, iPod, iWatch, iOS operating system, Safari browser *Mobile soft- and hardware for corporate clients* Strategic alliances Apple-IBM, Apple-SAP, Apple-Cisco *Cloud* iCloud *Internet of Things* Wearables, health and fitness, connected car	*Mobile hard- and software* Smartphone/tablet manufacturers, Amazon, Google (Android), Microsoft *Media* Google, Amazon, Netflix, Hulu, Spotify, media companies *Connected car* Google, car manufacturers *IT Services* Microsoft, Amazon, Google
Microsoft	Computer software/IT services	*Media* Games—Microsoft Studios, Xbox game console, MSN TV *Mobile soft- and hardware* Skype, Bing, MSN, Surface (tablet) *Social Networks* LinkedIn	*Mobile software* Google (Android); Apple (macOS, iOS); Apple-IBM *Media* Amazon, Google, Apple, game developers *IT services* Google, Apple, Amazon, IBM *Social networks* Facebook, Twitter, Xing, Google+

Source Annual Reports of the companies; media content analysis; own compilation on the territory of the classic media companies (film, music and book publishers), established game publishers (Microsoft, Sony and Nintendo) as well as web-based movie rental and streaming companies (Netflix, Hulu and Spotify). Apple (with iPod, iPad, iPhone and iWatch) and Amazon (with the Kindle e-book reader, Kindle Fire tablet and Fire TV stick) also offer, as a means to provide access to their content and services, complete and proprietary device families. Google, for its part, focuses on driving the spread of its open source mobile Android operating system, with which it establishes priority access to its users via the devices of other manufacturers (Annual Reports [Form 10-K] of the companies; media content analysis).

The second key trend, which is closely linked to the first trend, concerns the *dominance over the mobile internet*. This competition is fought out primarily between Google and Apple, whose operating systems are installed on over 90% of all mobile devices and which have by far the largest app stores. In addition, Amazon, which is already marketing a complete range of mobile devices and services, is likewise trying to join the ranks of the major players in this field—so much that it even engages in predatory pricing. Microsoft, even despite the acquisition of Nokia Devices, has not yet succeeded to make inroads into this field. In the meantime, the dominance of Google and Apple in the mobile devices market means that, unlike at the end of the 2000s, they can impose their rules on other device manufacturers and large telecommunication companies wishing to use their software or sell their devices. While Apple, with its advancement in the mobile internet market, aims primarily at marketing its hardware, Google's primary goal is to provide users, through the spread of its operating system and mobile browser, with priority access to its services (Annual Reports [Form 10-K] of the companies; media content analysis; Dolata and Schrape 2014).

In addition to these two major trends, two new markets have emerged over the last few years and are being pursued by the main internet groups (Amazon, Apple, Google and Microsoft) not only through acquisitions but also through strategic alliances. The first of these—comprising the third key trend—is the provision of *data storage, computing capacity and cloud services*. These offers and services can be used not only by individual internet users to store and retrieve their music, images, documents, contacts and programs from external computers but also by business customers who outsource entire internal data processing infrastructures onto the new platforms. Here, Apple and IBM have entered, in mid-2014, a strategic alliance designed to combine the offerings of mobile devices and services from Apple with the experience of IBM in the construction and management of company-internal data processing and communication structures. The aim of this alliance, alongside others with SAP and Cisco, is to, by way of devices, software and services, make the internal IT and communication structures of business customers more compatible with the mobile web. At the same time, this alliance serves to challenge Microsoft as a leader in the field of IT equipment and consulting for companies (media content analysis).

As a fourth key trend, especially Google, Apple and Amazon are increasingly pioneering fields that until recently have not been affected or determined by the internet. For example, Amazon and Google are each working on developing *package delivery drones*, which challenges the established structures of the logistics industry as well as the conventional parcel delivery companies. In addition, with the acquisition of the thermostat and smoke detector manufacturer Nest, Google has also entered the *smart home sector*, effectively moving into territory that has been in the hands of, for instance, Microsoft, Bosch kitchen and home appliances, and the network equipment provider Cisco. Apple, for its part, with the introduction of its iWatch in 2014, has also been venturing into the field of *wearables*, that is, body-wearable information technology, and health and fitness-related monitoring and tracking devices. Google and Apple are competing not only with each other but also with the established automobile companies for dominance in the *connected car* sector (media content analysis). Finally, all companies are engaged in seminal projects in the realm of artificial intelligence and *augmented reality*.

The commercial internet is thus characterized not only by strong merger trends but also by intense competition in all its essential segments—a situation that, for better or for worse, challenges the power of individual companies on a continuous basis. As we have demonstrated, this pressure is generated more so by the big companies as direct competitors than by commercially-oriented newcomers, open source projects or forms of commons-based peer production. Thus, the essential feature of today's competition in the commercial internet is fierce oligopolistic competition between the leading companies, which is carried out primarily through aggressive innovation and expansion strategies. In all the mentioned areas of business, Google, Apple and Amazon are currently the key players, with Facebook still in a consolidation phase and Microsoft largely consumed in a defensive battle. Under these conditions of oligopolistic competition, individual start-ups only have a chance of becoming significant (co-)players if they can occupy a completely new, not yet consolidated commercial field that is not on the radar of the established companies. Examples of the latter are the search engine market in the early 2000s, social networking one decade later, and the recent reconfiguration of the markets for online accommodation and car transportation services. However, start-ups that are innovative in fields that have already been appropriated, such as WhatsApp in the messaging service sector, are essentially easy prey to becoming bought out by the main players.

The expansion strategies of the internet companies are typically twofold. While the leading companies in other economic sectors often have drastically reduced the number of their business areas over the last two decades, instead focusing on a few core areas (such as the pharmaceutical industry, Dolata 2003, pp. 185–192), the internet companies are successively diversifying and expanding their reach. However, despite their diversification activities, none of them has managed to complement their core business with commercially viable new business areas to date. Although all five companies, and especially Google, Amazon and Apple, have through their expansion and acquisition strategies de facto become media groups with a broad offer of media content and services, all of them continue to generate the vast majority of their revenues and profits from their traditional core business (Table 1). Economically, Google and Facebook are still web-based advertising and marketing companies, Apple is still a leading provider of communications and consumer electronics, Microsoft is still a software company, and Amazon an internet retailer. Until now, the in part strong expansion and diversification into new business segments serves above all to enhance these companies' sociotechnical ecosystems, which are designed for the extensive and exclusive use by individual users as well as business customers. Nonetheless, this has not yet eclipsed the still enormous economic importance of their core business areas.

The second characteristic of these companies' innovation and expansion strategies can be summed up as "acquisition instead of cooperation." In other words, the examined companies do not, generally, obtain external know-how and penetrate into new business areas through cooperation with start-ups, as is the case in other high-tech sectors (Rothaermel 2001; Roijakkers and Hagedoorn 2006; Hagedoorn et al. 2000) but rather through the acquisition of companies whose resources and competences are integrated into the respective group.

4 Innovation: Closed Cores, Controlled Opening of Peripheries

The latter characteristic is also indicative of the companies' strong in-house orientation, in particular with regard to R&D, for which strategic alliances and cooperations are entered into only on rare occasions.

In general, in economic sectors characterized by oligopolistic structures and strong innovation dynamics, the struggle for dominance focuses primarily on achieving a competitive edge in research and the rapid marketing of innovations (Ahuja et al. 2008). This is particularly true of the commercial internet:

> R&D is the central input of production, not merely an episodic activity that affects the production process. Put differently, the R&D process and the production process are essentially the same thing for many products and services related to the internet and digital platforms. (Shelanski 2013, p. 1685)

Therefore, it is not surprising that all of the five internet companies are highly research-intensive, have large-scale R&D centers, and allocate a substantial portion of their staff to R&D (Table 1).[2] The central feature of the way in which they organize their R&D activities is not only a strong in-house orientation but also what has been termed *closed innovation* for some time now (Chesbrough 2003a, b; West et al. 2014). A significant portion of the products and services that characterize the internet today and which users are confronted with in rapid succession derives from internal research and is developed and produced under conditions of strict secrecy. Among these are Google's search algorithm; Facebook's social graph; Microsoft's software packages; Google and Facebook's data evaluation and advertising systems; Apple and Microsoft's operating systems; Apple and Amazon's device families;

---

[2]The, at first sight, very low percentage of R&D in Apple's total turnover (Table 1) should not be interpreted as a weakness. The group's product portfolio, to which its R&D is dedicated, is fairly small. Moreover, its exorbitant growth rate over the last 15 years—from $5.4 billion in 2001 to just under $230 billion in 2017—invariably dwarfs the R&D intensity (as a percentage of R&D expenditure in relation to total revenue) (Apple 2001, 2017).

Apple, Amazon and Google's cloud services; and Amazon's ordering and logistics systems. If and when know-how for proprietary developments is lacking, the companies rely on acquisitions of technology companies that offer the sought for resources (Table 3).

Microsoft explains, which could be representative of any of the other groups, the strong internal focus of its R&D activities as follows:

> We develop most of our products and services internally. Internal development allows us to maintain competitive advantages that come from product differentiation and closer technical control over our products and services. It also gives us the freedom to decide which modifications and enhancements are most important and when they should be implemented. [...] Generally, we also create product documentation internally. (Microsoft 2013, p. 8)

In a statement that could likewise have been issued by any of the other companies, Google points to the great importance of confidentiality and secrecy in its R&D activities and to which it commits both its staff and third parties:

> We rely on a combination of patent, trademark, copyright, and trade secret laws in the U.S. and other jurisdictions as well as confidentiality procedures and contractual provisions to protect our proprietary technology and our brand. We also enter into confidentiality and invention assignment agreements with our employees and consultants and confidentiality agreements with other third parties, and we rigorously control access to proprietary technology. (Google 2010, p. 16)

The *core of the innovation model* of the five internet companies is therefore a strong internal orientation of their R&D and the practice of those activities under quarantine-like conditions of extreme secrecy. The main reason for this is that the successful development and marketing of proprietary innovations on the internet markets comprises the basis for achieving competitive advantages over competitors. To this end, all companies seek to maintain utmost secrecy and control over their research activities and innovation projects, especially those crucial to their corporate strategy, and to secure the intellectual property rights of their products and services (Trott and Hartmann 2009; Braun and Herstatt 2008; Freedman 2012).

At the same time, however, there are also *controlled openings* at the edges of this closed system—especially in the form of relationships between the internet companies and open source communities as well as within the framework of the companies' own app stores.

All internet companies have long been benefiting from the adaptation of software developments that have been driven in the context of open source communities such as Linux, Mozilla or Apache (Lerner and Tirole 2002). Open source software is a constituent part of operating systems (such as macOS and iOS from Apple or Android from Google) and servers, of devices (such as the Apple iPhone or Kindle from Amazon), of tools for external developers, of preinstalled mobile app devices and of the cloud services offered by internet companies.[3] It is therefore important for

---

[3]For example, Google itself points to "the vital role of open source software plays at Google" (https://developers.google.-com/open-source/) and Apple emphasizes that "Open Source development [is] a key part of its ongoing software strategy" (https://www.apple.com/opensource/). Amazon too uses "tons of Linux, not only to power all the servers that it uses for retail but also for Amazon Web Services—and in its own Kindle Device" (Brockmeier 2011).

them to stay abreast of, and gain access to, the widely dispersed knowledge generated in the various open source communities. To this end, the companies employ a non-negligible number of people who are involved in open source development and who work in open source communities. They also participate, through their employees, in the big developer conferences of those communities and even contribute to the financing of open source projects and their foundations (West and O'Mahoney 2008). The Mozilla Foundation is funded by Google; the main sponsors of the Apache Software Foundation include Google, Microsoft and Facebook as platinum members with donations of more than $100,000 per year; and the Linux Foundation is financed by numerous large companies including Google, Amazon, Twitter and Samsung (Schrape 2017).

Dahlander and Gann (2010) refer to this aptly as inbound innovation sourcing. According to them, the companies' activities in the open software sector allow them to gain access to a wide range of external ideas and knowledge—unobstructed by formalized and contractually regulated cooperations and with comparatively little asked in return. The companies then exploit and utilize said ideas and knowledge for their internal R&D, a practice described as "parasitic actions by firms" by West and Lakhani (2008). Amazon, in particular, is described as a company "that harvests code from vast fields of open source software while obscuring its code donations and distancing itself from the wider world of computing" (Clark 2014).

Controlled openings also exist in the fast-growing field of software applications, or apps, that are tailored to mobile devices. Indeed, in today's market a mobile device would not be viable unless it comes with a broad range of apps. The central hubs for spreading mobile applications are Google and Apple, which, with well over one million apps each, have by far the largest app stores. Amazon is likewise active in this field, with its own app store that offers no less than one quarter of a million apps. It is obvious that only a fraction of this huge number of apps could possibly come from in-house development and that the companies rely on the work of countless external developers and companies. In no other area of business is the collaboration of the major internet companies with third-party providers as extensive as in the mobile apps field. Therefore, they have to maintain a new balance between control on the one hand and decentralized creative freedom on the other (Eaton et al. 2011; Schreyögg and Sydow 2010).

Nonetheless, these openings which the companies concede to are subjected to rigid control strategies. The app sector, as such, is not a bottom-up market that was initiated by countless developers but rather a top-down market established and developed mainly by Apple and Google. These companies control the app market as follows: they coordinate and monitor their app stores; define the licensing conditions and price structures; specify the criteria that an application must meet in order to be sold there; remove offers that do not appear opportune to them or that are classified as politically incorrect; co-determine, with their supporting software development kits, the appearance of the apps and the terms and conditions for using them; and contribute significantly to the success or failure of offers through the search algorithms in their stores. In addition, the companies resort to their app stores as a pool of ideas that they can draw on if need be. In recent years, Apple and Google have consistently integrated new application ideas into their own products or acquired promising emerging market players. For example, Google has purchased the apps Flutter (movement control), Sparrow (e-mail client) and Waze (social GPS); and Apple has purchased Siri (voice control), Cue (personal assistant) and Spotsetter (social maps) (Dolata and Schrape 2014, Table 3).

The internet companies are thus perceptive to their environments and systematically exploit external innovation impulses. They observe very closely what is happening in the open source communities; collaborate in open source projects; revert to a not insignificant degree to software and know-how developed there; outsource development activities when their own R&D capacities have reached their limits to external developers and companies; and regularly and systematically survey the wide field of start-up companies for interesting takeover targets.

However, a sustained opening-up of the essentially closed innovation model can hardly be observed. The companies thus continue to be characterized by a strong focus on proprietary developments, which mainly take place in their in-house R&D centers that are extremely sealed off from the outside world. In this way, the innovation model of the internet companies differs significantly from the patterns of collaborative technology and product development that are typical of other high-tech sectors. In sum, what became known in the 1990s as the *Networks of Innovators*—"The locus of innovation will be found in networks of learning, rather than in individual firms" (Powell et al. 1996, p. 116; Powell and Grodal 2005; Freeman 1991; Pittaway et al. 2004)—and which has since been relabeled as *Open Innovation*—"a distributed innovation process based on purposively managed knowledge flows across organizational boundaries" (Chesbrough and Bogers 2014; Chesbrough 2003a, b; West et al. 2014)—does not apply to the internet companies.

5   Power: Centralization, Control and Volatility

The above discussions provide us with an *overall picture* that has three main features.

First, the commercial internet is today dominated by a small number of internationally active companies and is characterized by a strong trend toward market concentration in all major segments. These processes are driven mainly by network effects, the establishment of company-specific sociotechnical ecosystems, and the extraordinary financial strength that the leading internet groups by now possess. Of course, the commercial internet is more than the sum of its leading companies. Similar to the classic economic sectors, it continues to be impacted by the dispersed activities of countless developers, start-ups and smaller companies who operate outside of its core structures.[4] This, of course, does not invalidate our *first finding* of a significant *hierarchization, market concentration and economic power structure*

---

[4]The automotive industry, for example, has numerous suppliers; and in the pharmaceutical industry there are the many R&D-intensive start-up companies that exist alongside and in cooperation with the large pharmaceutical companies.

in the commercial internet. Indeed, the prevailing notion in the early 2000s of the "internet economy"—in other words, a new form of business characterized by a multitude of new digital business opportunities, perfect markets, free competition and decentralized structures (Litan and Rivlin 2001; Anderson 2008)—has little to do with the reality of the commercial internet today.

Second, today's commercial internet is characterized by fierce rivalry at all levels. This applies not only to newly emerging segments, such as the search engine market in the early 2000s or, a decade later, the social networks sector, where an initial pool of competing start-ups would merge into one or two dominant groups. It also applies to segments that are already established and that have been subject to considerable market concentration, and which are the domains of individual companies. The internet companies act not only as established players who are primarily concerned with securing their respective domains but also as challengers who, with aggressive expansion strategies, endeavor to penetrate the domains of their fellow competitors and to continuously challenge positions of power. Thus, the intense oligopolistic competition which the established internet companies are subject to, both against one another and against communications, consumer electronics and media groups, does not change the high degree of concentration that is typical of the commercial internet. However, and constituting the *second finding*, it leads to a remarkable *volatility of acquired market and power positions*, which must be repeatedly defended and renewed in the face of the extremely rapid succession of innovation dynamics—and which cannot always be sustained.

Thirdly, the rivalries between the internet companies primarily concern innovative leads. The latter, even if only temporary, are acknowledged as a means to drive the ongoing development of software, devices, services, technical infrastructures and integrated ecosystems. The strategic importance of a group's own R&D is, accordingly, very high. The companies make intensive use of the dispersed knowledge and know-how that is emerging in open source communities, and also draw on the contributions of a large number of software developers and companies, for instance in the framework of their app stores. In the core area of competitively relevant innovation projects, however—this being the *third finding*—they are still in-house oriented; insist on utmost secrecy and sealed-off conditions for conducting their R&D and managing their knowledge base; and prefer a *closed innovation model* with which they seek to secure as much control as possible over their proprietary projects, products and services. Thus, overall their activities have little to do with open innovation or with the decentralization and democratization of innovation processes.

What, then, constitutes the power of the internet companies? Their power first manifests as an *economic power*, which is based on the superior economic resources of the companies—their financial strength, strong research capacity, market dominance as well as their ability to create, control and regulate own markets within their platforms—which they use against the competition and with which they can keep new competitors at bay.

In addition, internet companies are gradually broadening their *power over data*, namely by interlinking their range of cross-divisional offerings and by systematically matching and evaluating the resulting user traces. For example, the companies use their large volumes of data to create ever-more differentiated user profiles, which are applied to anticipate what users want—ideally even before the users themselves might acknowledge or express their own wants. These profiles also serve as an important input for their research and production and help to refine their products and services and to tailor these as closely as possible to user preferences (Shelanski 2013). Google's former CEO, Eric Schmidt, aptly expressed this in an interview during the Washington Ideas Forum in 2010 as follows:

> With your permission, you give us more information, if you give us information about who some of your friends are, we can probably use some of this information—again: with your permission—to improve the quality of our searches. [...] We don't need you to type at all. "Cause we know where you are—with your permission. We know where you've been—with your permission. We can more or less guess what you're thinking about. Now is that right over the line? [...] So we'll try to find that line to try to help you understand more about the world around you." (Eric Schmidt at Washington Ideas Forum, 1 October 2010, https:// www.youtube.com/watch?v=CeQsPSaitL0)

However, the power of internet companies is above all based on their ability to, by means of numerous and coordinated offers, design and shape the framework conditions of essential *social* contexts, be they consumer worlds, information and communication patterns or social relationship networks. No device, no software, no app store and no search, media, consumer or social platform is simply a neutral technical offering that allows users to design and redefine their content. At all times, the underlying technology incorporates rules, standards and instructions that impact the activities of users similarly to how social institutions influence people's behavior (Winner 1980; Lessig 1999).

This starts with, for example, the predefined user interfaces and default settings of the platforms, which are not usually changed by the users and which have a strong structuring effect on their actions insofar as they allow for certain activities while excluding others. The embedding of features such as the trending button on Twitter, emoticon buttons or the trending news function of Facebook are not just technical gadgets but rule-setting, action-orienting and opinion-forming structural elements. Socially constructed algorithms are used to determine what might be relevant, or not, for whom and to structure all information and interaction processes, to antici-pate user preferences and to make recommendations. Together with intra-company content moderation teams, algorithms function to decide on what is obscene, offen-sive, politically incorrect, erotic or pornographic—and to relegate or delete content accordingly. In this way, algorithms, forming the basis for any search, information, communication and interaction on these platforms, are highly political programs that construct distinct, selective and increasingly personalized social realities on the basis of social criteria that ultimately remain obscure to both the individual and the public (Just and Latzer 2017; Gillespie 2014; Van Dijck 2013; Pariser 2011).

This can be described as *infrastructural and rule-setting power*. In that the internet companies develop and provide the essential infrastructural foundations of the web and act as gatekeepers to access to the web, they become the main rule-setting and -controlling actors. As part of that function, they structure the online experience of individual users and collectives and prescribe framework conditions for their activities, whereby they ultimately influence users' behavior and actions. As companies that seek to have a socio-political vision and voice, they structure and shape large segments of private and public life on the web through the technically mediated social specifications of their offers—all below the radar of public perception and control. This means that they are not merely intermediaries, such as telephone companies, but are action-orienting and opinion-forming "curators of public discourse" (Gillespie 2010, p. 347).

In sum, the purview of the internet companies' power today includes, beyond the economic dominance of the commercial internet markets, a major influence on the constitution of the public in our societies—albeit without being limitless or absolute. After all, power is never simply a "thing" that one either has or does not have but rather the outcome of social relationships, and is therefore continuously subject to negotiation and contestation. This proposition applies to asymmetrically developed relationships in which subordinates always have specific resources and room for action with which they can irritate, influence or even challenge those in power (Giddens 1984).

This relational and dynamic view on power applies not only to the fierce rivalries in which the internet companies everywhere are entangled. Indeed, AOL, Yahoo, MySpace or Nokia are examples of how quickly market-dominant positions in this dynamic business can dissipate. The regulatory activities of national governments and of the European Community, too, can pose problems for internet companies, as shown by the political debates over the power of Google, Facebook and Apple. Finally, although the internet companies know far more about their users than vice versa, collective preferences and behaviors can nevertheless, when condensed into a mass phenomenon, impel said companies to make corrections or revisions of their strategic orientation, or can even induce existential crises.

In such turbulent environments as are typical for the (commercial) internet, the companies must continually work on optimizing and aligning their resources, competencies and scope of influence and on adapting themselves to rapidly changing conditions. If they fail to do so, within due time, they may see their power erode very quickly.

References

Ahuja, G., Lampert, C. M., & Tandon, V. (2008). Moving beyond Schumpeter: Management research on the determinants of technological innovation. *The Academy of Management Annals, 2*(1), 1–98.

Amazon.com Inc. (2013). *Annual Report 2012 (Form 10-K)*. United States Securities and Exchange Commission: Washington D.C.

Anderson, C. (2008). *The long tail. Why the future of business is selling less of more.* New York: Hachette Books.

Angwin, J. (2009). *Stealing MySpace: The battle to control the most popular website in America.* New York: Random House.

Apple Inc. (2001). *Annual Report 2001 (Form 10-K)*. United States Securities and Exchange Commission: Washington D.C.

Apple Inc. (2017). *Annual Report 2017 (Form 10-K)*. United States Securities and Exchange Commission: Washington D.C.

Arthur, C. (2012). *Digital wars: Apple, Google, Microsoft and the battle for the internet*. London/Philadelphia: Kogan Page.

Atkinson, R. D., Ezell, S. J., Andes, S. M., Castro, D. D., & Bennett, R. (2010). *The internet economy 25 years after. Transforming commerce & life*. Washington D.C.: The Information Technology & Innovation Foundation.

Barabasi, A.-L., & Bonabeau, E. (2003). Scale-free networks. *Scientific American, 5*, 50–59.

Benkler, Y. (2006). *The wealth of networks: How social production transforms markets and freedom*. New Haven/London: Yale University Press.

Braun, V., & Herstatt, C. (2008). The freedom-fighters: How incumbent corporations are attempting to control user-innovation. *International Journal of Innovation Management, 12*(3), 543–572.

Brockmeier, J. (2011). Does Amazon "owe" open source? Maybe a little. *Network World*. https://www.networkworld.com/article/2229358/opensource-subnet/does-amazon–owe–open-source–maybe-a-little.html. Accessed 5 February 2018.

Chesbrough, H. W. (2003a). The era of open innovation. *MIT Sloan Management Review, 44*(3), 35–41.

Chesbrough, H. W. (2003b). *Open innovation: The new imperative for creating and profiting from technology*. Boston: Harvard Business School Press.

Chesbrough, H. W., & Bogers, M. (2014). Explicating open innovation: Clarifying an emerging paradigm for understanding innovation. In H. W. Chesbrough, W. Vanhaverbeke, & J. West (Eds.), *New frontiers in open innovation* (pp. 3–27). Oxford: Oxford University Press.

Clark, J. (2014). Amazon's "schizophrenic" open source selfishness scares off potential talent, say insiders. *The Register*. http://www.theregister.co.uk/2014/01/22/amazon_open_source_investigation/. Accessed 5 February 2018.

Dahlander, L., & Gann, D. M. (2010). How open is innovation? *Research Policy, 39*, 699–709.

Dolata, U. (2003). *Unternehmen Technik. Akteure, Interaktionsmuster und strukturelle Kontexte der Technikentwicklung: Ein Theorierahmen*. Berlin: Edition Sigma.

Dolata, U. (2013). *The transformative capacity of new technologies. A theory of sociotechnical change*. London/New York: Routledge.

Dolata, U., & Schrape, J.-F. (2013). Medien in Transformation. Radikaler Wandel als schrittweise Rekonfiguration. In U. Dolata & J.-F. Schrape (Eds.), *Internet, Mobile Devices und die Transformation der Medien. Radikaler Wandel als schrittweise Rekonfiguration* (pp. 9–36). Berlin: Edition Sigma.

Dolata, U., & Schrape, J.-F. (2014). App-Economy: Demokratisierung des Software-Marktes? *Technikfolgenabschätzung – Theorie und Praxis, 23*(2), 76–80.

Dolata, U., & Schrape, J.-F. (2016). Masses, crowds, communities, movements. Collective action in the internet age. *Social Movement Studies, 15*(1), 1–18.

Eaton, B., Elaluf-Calderwood, S., Sörensen, C., & Yoo, Y. (2011). *Dynamic structures of control and generativity in digital ecosystem service innovation: The cases of the Apple and Google mobile app stores*. Working Paper Series 183. London: LSE Innovation Systems and Innovation Group.

Evans, D. S. (2008). The economics of the online advertising industry. *Review of Network Economics, 7*(3), 359–391.

Facebook Inc. (2018). *Annual Report 2017 (Form 10-K)*. United States Securities and Exchange Commission: Washington D.C.

Fortune (2017). *Fortune 500 2016*. http://fortune.com/fortune500/list. Accessed 5 February 2018.

Freedman, D. (2012). Web 2.0 and the death of the blockbuster economy. In J. Curran, N. Fenton, & D. Freedman (Eds.), *Misunderstanding the internet* (pp. 69–94). London/New York: Routledge.

Freeman, C. (1991). Networks of innovators: A synthesis of research issues. *Research Policy, 20*, 499–514.

Garcia, C. (2017). *US ecommerce sales 2017. The top 10 companies. eMarketer Report*. eMarketer.

Giddens, A. (1984). *The constitution of society*. Cambridge: Polity Press.

Gillespie, T. (2010). The politics of "platforms". *New Media & Society, 12*(3), 347–364.

Gillespie, T. (2014). The relevance of algorithms. In T. Gillespie, P. Boczkowski, & K. Foot (Eds.), *Media technologies. Essays on communication, materiality, and society* (pp. 167–194). Cambridge: MIT Press.

Google Inc. (2010). *Annual Report 2009 (Form 10-K)*. United States Securities and Exchange Commission: Washington D.C.

Hagedoorn, J., Link, A. N., & Vonortas, N. S. (2000). Research partnerships. *Research Policy, 29*, 567–586.

Haucap, J., & Heimeshoff, U. (2014). Google, Facebook, Amazon, eBay: Is the internet driving competition or market monopolization? *International Economics and Economic Policy, 11*(1–2), 49–61.

Haucap, J., & Wenzel, T. (2011). Wettbewerb im Internet: Was ist online anders als offline? *Zeitschrift für Wirtschaftspolitik, 60*(2), 200–211.

Hong, A., Bhattacharyya, D., & Geis, G. T. (2013). The role of M&A in market convergence: Amazon, Apple, Google and Microsoft. *Global Economy and Finance Journal, 6*(1), 53–73.

IDC (2017). *Worldwide Quarterly Mobile Phone Tracker*. https://www.idc.com/tracker/showproductinfo.jsp?prod_id=37. Accessed 27 April 2017.

Just, N., & Latzer, M. (2017). Governance by algorithms: Reality construction by algorithmic selection on the internet. *Media, Culture and Society, 39*(2), 238–258.

Kenney, M., & Zysman, J. (2016). The rise of the platform economy. *Issues in Science and Technology, Spring, 2016*, 61–69.

Kirchner, S., & Beyer, J. (2016). Die Plattformlogik als digitale Marktordnung. Wie die Digitalisierung Kopplungen von Unternehmen löst und Märkte transformiert. *Zeitschrift für Soziologie, 45*(5), 324–339.

Kirkpatrick, D. (2010). *The Facebook effect. The inside story of the company that is connecting the world*. New York: Simon & Schuster.

Lerner, J., & Tirole, J. (2002). Some simple economics of open source. *The Journal of Industrial Economics, 50*(2), 197–233.

Lessig, L. (1999). *CODE and other laws of cyberspace*. New York: Basic Books.

Litan, R. E., & Rivlin, A. M. (Eds.). (2001). *The economic payoff from the internet revolution*. Brookings Institution: Washington D.C.

Mellahi, K., & Wilkinson, A. (2004). Organizational failure: A critique of recent research and a proposed integrative framework. *International Journal of Management Reviews, 5/6*(1), 21–41.

Microsoft Corporation. (2013). *Annual Report 2013 (Form 10-K)*. United States Securities and Exchange Commission: Washington D.C.

Monopolkommission. (2014). *Hauptgutachten 2012/2013. Eine Wettbewerbsordnung für die Finanzmärkte*. Baden-Baden: Nomos.

National Retail Federation. (2017a). *Top 50 e-retailers, 2015*. https://nrf.com/2017-top-50-e-retailers-chart Accessed 5 February 2018.

National Retail Federation. (2017b). *Top 100 retailers chart, 2017*. https://stores.org/stores-top-retailers-2017/. Accessed 5 February 2018.

Netmarketshare. (2017a). *Search engine market share (desktop and mobile/tablet)*. http://netmarketshare.com/. Accessed 5 February 2018.

Netmarketshare. (2017b). *Operating system market share (mobile/tablet)*. https://www.netmarketshare.com/ Accessed 5 February 2018.

Pariser, E. (2011). *The filter bubble. What the internet is hiding from you*. New York: Penguin Press.

Pittaway, L., Robertson, M., Munir, K., Denyer, D., & Neely, A. (2004). Networking and innovation: A systematic review of the evidence. *International Journal of Management Reviews, 5/6*(3&4), 137–168.

Pollock, R. (2010). Is Google the next Microsoft: Competition, welfare and regulation in online research. *Review of Network Economics, 9*(4), Article 4.

Powell, W. W., & Grodal, S. (2005). Networks of innovators. In J. Fagerberg, D. C. Mowery, & R. Nelson (Eds.), *The Oxford handbook of innovation* (pp. 56–85). Oxford: Oxford University Press.

Powell, W. W., Koput, K. W., & Smith-Doerr, L. (1996, March). Interorganizational collaboration and the locus of innovation: Networks of learning in biotechnology. *Administrative Science Quarterly,* 116–145.

PricewaterhouseCoopers. (2016). *IAB internet advertising revenue report. 2015 full year results.* New York: PwC.

PricewaterhouseCoopers. (2017). *IAB internet advertising revenue report. 2016 full year results.* New York: PwC.

Rochet, J.-C., & Tirole, J. (2003). Platform competition in two-sided markets. *Journal of the European Economic Association, 1*(4), 990–1029.

Roijakkers, N., & Hagedoorn, J. (2006). Inter-firm partnering in pharmaceutical biotechnology since 1975: Trends, patterns, and networks. *Research Policy, 35,* 431–446.

Rothaermel, F. T. (2001). Incumbent's advantage through exploiting complementary assets via interfirm cooperation. *Strategic Management Journal, 22*(6/7), 687–699.

Schrape, J.-F. (2017). Open-source projects as incubators of innovation: From niche phenomenon to integral part of the industry. *Convergence. The International Journal of Research into New Media Technologies.* OnlineFirst. http://journals.sagepub.com/doi/abs/10.1177/1354856517735795.

Schreyögg, G., & Sydow, J. (2010). Organizing for fluidity? Dilemmas of new organizational forms. *Organization Science, 21*(6), 1251–1262.

Shapiro, C., & Varian, H. R. (1999). *Information rules. A strategic guide to the network economy.* Boston: Harvard Business School Press.

Shelanski, H. E. (2013). Information, innovation, and competition policy for the internet. *University of Pennsylvania Law Review, 161,* 1663–1705.

Srnicek, N. (2017). *Platform capitalism.* Cambridge/Malden: Polity Press.

Stone, B. (2013). *The everything store. Jeff Bezos and the age of Amazon.* Little, Brown and Company: New York.

Tapscott, D., & Williams, A. D. (2006). *Wikinomics: How mass collaboration changes everything.* New York: Portfolio.

Trott, P., & Hartmann, D. (2009). Why "open innovation" is old wine in new bottles. *International Journal of Innovation Management, 13*(4), 715–736.

Van Dijck, J. (2013). *The culture of connectivity. A critical history of social media.* Oxford: Oxford University Press.

von Hippel, E. (2005). *Democratizing innovation.* Cambridge: MIT Press.

West, J., & Lakhani, K. R. (2008). Getting clear about communities in open innovation. *Industry & Innovation, 15*(2), 223–231.

West, J., & O'Mahoney, S. (2008). The role of participation architecture in growing sponsored open source communities. *Industry & Innovation, 15*(2), 145–168.

West, J., Salter, A., Vanhaverbeke, W., & Chresbrough, H. (2014). Open innovation: The next decade. *Research Policy, 43,* 805–811.

Winner, L. (1980). Do artifacts have politics? *Daedalus, 109*(1), 121–136.